Life is fo

Patience Strong

Life is for Living

Thoughts on Practical Psychology

FREDERICK MULLER LTD

First published in Great Britain in 1971 by
Frederick Muller Ltd, London, NW2 6LE

Copyright © 1971 Patience Strong

Reprinted 1973

For Rupert Crew
in appreciation

Printed in Great Britain by The Anchor Press Ltd,
and bound by Wm. Brendon & Son Ltd,
both of Tiptree, Essex

ISBN 0 584 10762 5

TO THE MEMORY OF CHARLES WASE whose work as healer and lecturer flashed a new light on old dogmas by teaching people how to attain health, happiness and harmony through a simple method of re-educating the subconscious mind.

For many years I have felt that there was a need to restate the ideas and ideals of writers like Emerson, Thoreau, Prentice Mulford, Ralph Waldo Trine and Mary Baker Eddy, founder of the world wide church of Christian Science, and this is an attempt to distil out of their writings some essential truth which will have meaning and relevance to the problems of the present. As John Wesley in his day galvanised the faith into life by preaching in the new language of evangelicalism, those American writers shaped the new thought of the new world at the beginning of the century at a time when orthodox Christianity was coming under fire from the rationalists. It was they who built the first bridges between religion and psychology, and history may well attest that in so doing they saved their own and future generations from falling disastrously between the two stools of a formal Anglo-Catholicism on the one hand and a sterile humanism on the other.

In the work of the Englishman, Charles Wase, I discovered what seemed to be a synthesis of the many systems of healing and regeneration practised here and in America and I have tried to put something of his tremendous life-giving message between the covers of a small book, the message which he called the gospel of healthy-mindedness.

Life is for Living

Life is for living so live it and see
   How great and how beautiful living can be,
Life is for letting the glory get through
   Shedding its light upon all that you do.
Life's more than suffering, sorrow and sin
   Life is for building the kingdom within.
Christ, the Restorer, empowers you this day,
   Loving and living the Galilee way,
Your world to renew and your self to make whole,
   Healing the body, the mind and the soul.

PATIENCE STRONG

Contents

Introduction

Most normal people want to be healthy, happy and successful yet so many are unhealthy, unhappy and dissatisfied. They may not be sick but they are not fit. They may not be really miserable but they are not bubbling over with the joy of life. They may not be in financial difficulties but they never seem to have sufficient for their daily requirements. In other words, they are only half alive.

Health, happiness and success are three separate aspects of the one comprehensive word: harmony. You cannot make music unless you are prepared to accept and co-operate with the basic laws of harmony and if you choose to disregard them the result is discord. How can you play life like an instrument so that it produces harmony? Is there a simple way of making this kind of music in a world full of discordant situations, disease and death? It can be done, but just as you cannot hope to be proficient at the piano until you have mastered your five-finger exercises you must be prepared to practise the simple scales in the art of living if you are to live it victoriously. You have to accept the proposition that discord and disease have no part in the ideal life. They are distortions of reality, for they misrepresent the true nature of man as the distorting mirrors at a fun fair reflect not the true image but a misshapen monstrosity.

In this book I have attempted to suggest a few simple directions for right thinking so that you can train yourself to be the sort of person you want to be and, indeed, the sort of person you must be if you are to claim your rightful heritage of health, happiness and harmony.

It is easy to diagnose the ills of life and to prescribe remedies but not so easy to explain how these remedies work. The prescription must be taken on trust without demanding theological and metaphysical explanations as to how and why they work. It is not necessary to understand the mechanism of a car in order to drive it, nor do you have to study electro-dynamics before you can switch on an electric light so you do not have to know how spiritual power operates in order to harness and use it.

There is nothing here which is not backed by the authority of the Bible. It is an attempt to reduce some of its great truths to terms in which they can be understood and demonstrated in a practical way.

THE RE-EDUCATION OF THE
SUBCONSCIOUS MIND

As health and happiness depend so largely upon your habitual thinking it is necessary to cultivate right habits of thought, and the only way to do this is through the re-education of the subconscious mind.

First, it is necessary to understand that the mind works on two layers of consciousness, the objective and the subjective, and for purposes of simplification it can be likened to water in a well. On the surface is the water that you can see because it reflects light. This is the part of the mind used superficially in the day to day business of living. Its responses are almost mechanical. All the time you are awake it is busy assimilating facts and transmitting messages: a truly marvellous piece of mechanism. Below this lies the subconscious mind, the underground reservoir from which spring all your impulses, instincts and feelings. This reservoir opens out at its sources into what Emerson called the Superconscious and what the mystics and theologians call God, and at the very depths of your being you are connected with this Divine inflow.

Here in the subconscious lies all that you need in the way of wisdom, inspiration, health and energy.

All the attributes of deity can be drawn upon through the subconscious mind if you let down the bucket in faith, never doubting. But we are content with so little in spite of the inexhaustible supply. We put up with half a life instead of going all out for the real thing. It is almost as if we were afraid of asking too much of life, afraid of freedom, afraid of living to the full.

How to set about exploring the possibilities of re-educating the part of the mind that moulds your life and shapes your personality? The acquiring of text-book knowledge at school is not education in the true sense of the word. Education begins when, independent of State or family, you launch out into the world and really get to grips with life and its problems, and in the course of this training in the university of living you accumulate all kinds of rubbish just as in a house the attic is usually stacked with junk. Take care not to overload the objective mind with too much useless information. Simplify your philosophy as far as you can and the process of re-educating the subconscious will be that much easier.

Nobody knows how the mind ticks. Scientists can devise a way of getting to the moon, but no so-called scientific expert can tell you what a thought is, where it comes from and where it goes.

Hamlet started with a thought. Every invention began with an idea in somebody's mind. Thought is creation and thought is power. We know that the influence of thought can be dynamic, destructive, beneficent or evil according to the will that controls and directs it. Within yourself you have the power to be what you want to be and to do what you want to do but you must learn to use that power wisely and carefully. Misuse can be dangerous.

Every moment of your waking life you are subject to the power of thought, your own and the thoughts of others. From every direction the brain is bombarded with thoughts. Suggestions and impressions seep down into the subconscious and become the formative stuff out of which your character evolves, so it is necessary to have a periodic check on what is passing down into the subconscious mind. It is possible to impress the subconscious with the ideas which you wish to see expressed in yourself and in your circumstances and this can be done only by daily and persistent training. It has no intelligence of its own. It can express only that which is suggested by the objective mind and enforced by the will. It can be influenced and conditioned to react in whatever way you desire and if you train it to work for you along the lines of health, happiness, wisdom and harmony, you will gradually find that your whole mentality will be coloured by these positive reactions.

It must always be remembered that you are enveloped in the atmosphere of the Superconscious just as the earth is surrounded by the ether. This all embracing power for good in which you live and move and have your being can be expressed in your life by the extent to which you can co-operate with it through the medium of your mind.

Begin now to educate your subconscious mind into acceptance of this wonderful fact. It is for you to decide whether you want to continue to put up with the half-life of poor health and unhappy living conditions or whether you are prepared to take the step that will bring you out of the shadows and into the sunshine of a radiant life of health and fulfilment. If the latter, the moment to start is now. Resolve from now on to feed into your subconscious mind thoughts which tend towards harmony, health, happiness and peace.

Physical health is a reflection of your mental condition. Moods, emotions and attitudes of mind affect the tone of the body for good or ill. Every destructive thought produces its own kind of disease because it weakens and destroys instead of strengthening and building up. Do not be afraid of the word disease. It means nothing more than a state of being not at ease as a consequence of transgressing at some point against the laws of life. Wrong habits of eating, living and thinking all, in time, produce their inevitable results and the sufferer is caught in the working out of the inexorable laws of cause and effect.

It is comforting to reflect that your health does not depend upon medical science for its maintenance. It is dependent upon something more reliable; it is based on law, the law that like attracts like. The mind is coloured and conditioned by the matters with which it is chiefly concerned. If it is engaged continually with thoughts of ill-health, resentment, depression or fear it will absorb them into itself and sooner or later in one form or another these mental conditions will be externalised in the body. By the same process thoughts of health, love, goodwill and peace will have a beneficial effect upon the self-regulating mechanism that keeps the body fit and unimpaired as God meant it to be.

If you wish to make an elementary test of the practical way in which you can train and use the subconscious mind you can ask it to wake you up at a certain time and you will find, with practice, that such efficiency can be achieved. It will also act like a good secretary and rummage about in the archives of your memory to find some piece of mislaid knowledge. You may say you have forgotten a name or a thing, but leave it to your subconscious mind and when you are least expecting it the information will be forthcoming. You may have forgotten all about it but everything you want is there. Trust it and train it to work for you for good.

Some years ago Coué, a French chemist, achieved a not inconsiderable success with his famous formula, 'Every day and in every way I am getting better and better'. This simple system of auto-suggestion was based on acceptance of the fact that the subconscious mind is receptive and responsive to repeated suggestions which are eventually manifested in the body because the body is a part of the same being. Who can say where lies the division between mind and matter?

Train yourself to react to every circumstance in a positive and life-affirming way. Deny whatever tends towards poverty, defeat or disease. You will have many failures. Time and again you will be caught off your guard, but do not give up. Counter every suggestion with a positive affirmation of good and you will gradually establish the habit of reacting constructively to everything that happens, pleasant or unpleasant. When this way of thinking has hardened into habit the subconscious will not need to be reminded how it must react. It will make the right response to all problems you meet in the course of a day.

In the closing chapters of this book there are some suggested affirmations for daily use in the practical application of the principles involved in the process of re-educating the subconscious mind for the attainment of health, happiness and harmony, but it must be borne in mind that these mental exercises must be performed regularly. A fixed time should be set aside each morning and evening, or whenever else is convenient, but at any time of the day and whatever you are doing you can be practising. The more you repeat a certain phrase the more deeply will it form the track of habit and it is habitual thinking that brings the best and quickest results. Quietly and with confidence affirm that you are feeling better and in a few days you will feel a new sense of well-being glowing within you. Your step will be lighter, your eye brighter and your brain more alert because there is this power working within you that wants to express itself as health and happiness.

Give yourself a chance to live life as it wants to be lived. Refuse to accept a substitute for the glorious life that God wants you to enjoy in the marvellous body with which he has provided you. And remember that your mind is not an isolated unit working in a vacuum.

It is a part of the universal whole, an active cell in what Richard Jeffries referred to as the cosmos of thought, a self-conscious individual surrounded and sustained by what is described by Teilhard de Chardin as *Le Milieu Divin*. Realise the reality of this as you go about your daily affairs and nothing will be commonplace or uninteresting. Everything will be charged with significance and illuminated by a light not of this world. And when you have glimpsed something of this exciting aspect of life you will know that you are on the way to becoming alive in a sense that you never experienced before.

Cultivating the Yes-to-life attitude is not just a means of making living easier and more enjoyable and yourself happier and more efficient, it is literally a matter of life and death because the habit of saying 'No' to life induces a state of mental anaemia which in its final stages results in spiritual extinction. What you are at the moment before the spirit leaves the body is what you will be when you pass into the next phase of your evolution, declining into nothingness or progressing towards perfection according to the direction in which your thoughts have tended during your life on earth.

Death changes nothing except the outer garment. Only what is good in your character survives, the bad dies with your body so that survival is dependent upon the substance and constitution of the soul. A starved and stunted soul is a mere shadow of what it ought to be and a shadow cannot establish its identity.

There is nothing in the Bible that supports the idea

of automatic immortality. Paul said that the gift of
God is eternal life through Jesus Christ, our Lord, so
it is a gift to be rejected or received. The Master
simplified it by making faith in Him the gate of everlasting life. All that is required of us is the grace of
acceptance. This underlines the necessity of orientat-
ing the subconscious mind towards what is happy and
heavenly, and deepening the tracks of habitual thought
along the lines of faith, for the opening chords of the
next movement of the symphony of your life will be
played in the key to which the instrument has been
tuned. To live 'in tune with the infinite' is to live the
life of the kingdom of heaven here and now.

[2]

MIND IS MASTER

Because you are master in your own mental household you are able to control what you eat, what you
think and what you do, but it is not the autocratic
control of tyranny because you never lose sight of the
fact that you are a threefold being: mind, body and
spirit. You control the appetites of the physical for its
good, knowing that mind, body and soul must work
together in loving co-operation if they are to function
harmoniously. Having realised this basic fact it is safe
to allow your mind to exercise its mastery over anything that tends towards disease, disintegration or
defeat.

Within you lies the power to attract not only people
but circumstances. The kind of people who are drawn
into your aura and the circumstances you attract
around yourself depend on the nature of the thoughts
which predominate in your mind. Imagine yourself to
be at the centre of a field of magnetic energy. By the
operation of psychic suction power you are always
drawing towards yourself something which corres-
ponds to your inmost thoughts. It follows then that if
you live continually in a mental atmosphere of ill-

health, pessimism and poverty, you are bound to get onto the same wavelength with those who are similarly inclined. Thus you will become caught up in a spider's web of negative conditions. And the suction power works in reverse. Not only are you drawing adverse circumstances towards you, but you yourself are being drawn into the magnetic field of those who are on the same wavelength.

The opposite is true. If your mental attitude towards life is healthy, optimistic and constructive you will be drawn into contact with kindred spirits and gravitate towards conditions which are in harmony with your own hopes and desires.

When first you wake in the morning set your thoughts in the right direction. Start the day in a mood of joyous anticipation. Tell yourself that something wonderful is going to happen and expect it to happen. Translate hope into faith. 'This is the day that the Lord hath made. I will rejoice and be glad in it.' So said the Psalmist. It is your day. Make what you will of it best or worst. The choice is yours. Mind is master.

Within you lies the power of saying 'Yes' to life. Welcome whatever comes at you during the day as an opportunity of demonstrating this wonderful power within. Over and over again tell yourself that all is well and that everything is working itself out for your ultimate good. Do not be deflected from your course by difficult people or disrupting circumstances. Assert the supremacy of good over evil. Remember that this power within you has no intelligence of its own. Like electricity, it must be harnessed in order to be used.

It is for you to direct the great forces which are there and to channel them into the right stream. That is why you must never cease to affirm what is positive and health-giving.

If you live in a state of vague vacillation you cannot expect to get positive results from your daily affirmations of health, happiness and harmony. To drift through the world without faith in yourself and without the compass of a religious faith is to invite disaster. Like a ship without a rudder you will be tossed about in the chaotic storms caused by conflicting thought-waves and you will live your life at the mercy of circumstances instead of in control of them.

This is not mere academic speculation. Put these ideas into practice and you will find that a lovely and exciting new world opens out before you at the beginning of every new day. Christ said, 'The kingdom of heaven is within you'. That puts the whole truth about life neatly into a nutshell. In this kingdom within there is surely no room for any mental or physical states of dis-ease. This wonderful inner kingdom of health and happiness is yours for the finding, so begin now to bring it into being, remembering that our Lord said, 'Seek and ye shall find. Knock and it shall be opened unto you. Ask and ye shall receive.'

You have this Divine promise of success, so what are you waiting for? Commence today to live this new life. Claim it as your inheritance and make it your business to become all that you are capable of being within the framework of what God wills for you.

To accept the idea that there is an appointed part

for you to play in life that none but you can play is not
to be a fatalist. The right of choice still lies with you.
It is for you to say whether you are going to be content
with living on the lower levels of life or whether you
are going to identify yourself with something higher.
The more you affirm your belief in what is good and
strive to put your ideals into practice the more surely
you will be led along the right path, the path to fulfilment of your legitimate desires. But when these desires
emerge as realities do not forget to give God the glory.
Never think that you, personally, have wrought the
miracle. You have merely put into operation the
machinery of the Divine law of cause and effect.

Everything lives and breathes at a different rate of
vibration: trees, flowers, stones, animals and humans.
It was said once that God sleeps in the mineral,
dreams in the animal and wakes in man. It cannot be
denied that health is man's natural endowment. If
disease had been part of the Divine creation our Lord
would never have gone about from town to town healing the sick, cleansing the leper, curing the lame, the
blind, the deaf and the dumb.

Every miracle was a demonstration of the fact that
a sick man is an unnatural phenomenon. He does not
reflect the truth that man was made in the image and
likeness of his Creator. The restoration to health puts
him back into a right relationship to God. Surely then
it is right to will to be well.

What about cancer, heart failure, bronchitis, rheu-
matism and all the other scourges with which modern
man is afflicted? How can the mastery of the mind help

the unfortunate victims of organic disease? There is indeed a point at which the exercise of the will can arrest the forces of destruction and strengthen resistance to their attacks. For instance, what you eat and drink comes within the jurisdiction of the will. Overloading the system with too much food, or food of the wrong kind, sets up toxic conditions which give rise to all kinds of ailments. The will also takes over in matters arising out of decisions regarding treatment if medical science has failed to effect a cure. There have been many cases of the curing of malignant disease by unorthodox methods of treatment which are frowned upon by the professional hierarchy, and the patient or the patient's relatives have had to decide whether to put their trust in drugs, deep ray therapy, surgery etcetera or in methods which do not conform to the orthodox line. Autogenous vaccination and scientific dieting are two methods of treating cancer which have been effective in terminal cases, but someone has to make the vital decision and it takes courage to stand up to the juggernaut of medical prejudice.

It is an incontrovertible fact that we have in our bodies a built-in capacity to resist disease supported by an army of defenders whose job it is to rush to the point of attack by microbial invasion. The body manufactures its own antiseptics but it can deal only with a reasonable amount of toxic substances. Fasting gives it an opportunity to remarshal its forces of resistance. But these issues have to do with curing disease and the purpose of this book is concerned with preventing it through the training of the subconscious mind.

It is your duty to do all that you can to keep the natural defences of the body in order by maintaining good health, and anything that helps you along these lines should be given serious consideration.

Repeated affirmations of peace and harmony ease the mental tensions that lead to a breakdown in the nervous system. Overstrained nerves can weaken the will even to the point of a complete breakdown of the personality resulting in loss of memory or chronic melancholia. Painful crises of this kind do not occur in a mind that has been permeated through and through with quiet positive thoughts that help to establish a calm attitude towards life and maintain equilibrium.

We all live under pressure these days and are in need of tranquillisation, not by drugs which, in the long run, are harmful, but by quietening the nerves through the realisation of the peace which lies below the surface of trouble and turmoil. No matter how busy you are or how short of time you must make time to do this, for by so doing you will achieve the kind of life on which you are dependent for health, happiness and harmony. Let nothing prevent or deter you from devoting time each day to this vital meditation for it is truly a matter of life or death to condition yourself to become receptive to the good that is flowing towards you. However rich you may be, however healthy or however clever you cannot afford to cut yourself off from this stream of Providence. We all need to be open to the infinite life that embraces all blessings. We need it as we need air, water, light and exercise.

It is better to prevent an evil than to have to set

about fighting it if it comes, so look upon your daily meditations as time well spent, an investment for the future. At first it may seem a sacrifice of your time, sometimes perhaps an interruption, but as you progress and find yourself becoming more alive, healthier and more efficient, your mental exercises will cease to seem a sacrifice. You will look forward to them with joy as a hungry man anticipates a meal.

The therapy of silence is no mere figment of the imagination. It is a very real thing, so give yourself up to it as a swimmer gives himself up to the water, trusting in its buoyancy. You will be carried through the day on a great wave of well-being no matter what you come up against in the way of adverse circumstances. 'Count it all joy', said Paul. There is no better or more up-to-date textbook than the New Testament on the subject of practical psychology. If it were studied regularly and its meanings imbibed thoroughly the psychiatrists would soon be out of business and half the beds in our hospitals would not be occupied by patients suffering from nervous and mental disorders.

It is not scientific to dismiss a theory without investigation nor is it reasonable to condemn anything without giving it a trial. You do not have to understand how a computer works before making it work for you so do not refuse to experiment with this method of training the subconscious mind because, intellectually, you are incapable of understanding how it works. If you are serious you will not be interested in the mechanics of it, but in results.

When the writer of the Proverbs said, 'As he thinketh in his heart, so is he' he was saying what students of practical psychology are saying today: that whatever is fed into the subconscious becomes manifest externally as reality.

[3]

YOU MAKE YOUR OWN FACE

The late Dr Charles Wase, founder of the British School of Practical Psychology in the years which followed the First World War, based much of his teaching on the belief held by the Yogis of India, that we become like that upon which the mind dwells. In other words, the mind takes on the likeness of that which it contemplates and as facial expressions reflect mental conditions it follows that your appearance is largely dependent upon the nature of your thoughts. This being so, how necessary it is to correct wrong habits of thinking. If you are constantly under emotional strain it will eventually show in your face. If your thoughts are invariably occupied with worrying over things that do not really matter it will not be long before you develop a crease between the eyes. What you are is written on your face for all the world to see. No amount of cosmetics can cover it and no method of massage can smoothe away the tell-tale lines.

A look of youthfulness has nothing much to do with the date on your birth certificate. It is not the number of years that makes you look young or old, it is the attitude to the whole of life that makes all the difference. A gay spirit keeps the eye bright. A glad and grateful heart will quicken the step and as you walk out gaily and courageously into the beginning of every new day your movements will improve the circulation of the blood, which will glow in your cheeks.

Nothing wears the face out more than tension. Strain, fatigue and ill-humour are the enemies of beauty in a woman and of good looks in a man, so if you want to make yourself a pleasing face that will not only please others but last you a lifetime you must begin at once to mould it from within by the creative power of right thinking.

Know your enemies. The enemies of your face are legion; some of the most subtle and dangerous ones are self-pity, impatience, irritability, bad feelings towards others. These are some of the factors that are in league with time to make you look old and tired.

Be careful not to let these negative emotional responses become so habitual that they begin to play havoc with your face. The destructive process is so insidious that it may take some time for you to realise what is happening.

If this is the case there is not a moment to be lost. You must set about the immediate reconstruction of your whole mechanism. Resolve to control your responses. When anyone upsets you, count ten. Pause before you make the sharp retort. If you are feeling unwell meet it with a positive declaration that it is only a passing thing. You are getting better. Tomorrow you will be well. If not tomorrow then the next day. Form the habit of countering every adverse thought as it comes up.

If fear makes a rush at you take a firm stand against it in a spirit of hopefulness. If you have been badly treated and are feeling indignant remember that you must not indulge in feelings of resentment nor must you allow it to sink down into your subconscious as a harboured grievance. This is more than you dare do. Grievances have a way of becoming externalised in the body as an ailment or in the face as an expression. Skin is the outer covering of the bone structure and is in a state of perpetual renewal, but your bone arrangement is permanent. You carry your own skeleton around with you under the envelope of your skin, but in some mysterious way this skin is fictile under the plastic pressures of feelings and emotions.

This malleability of the face is not something that can be explained in precise terms so you do not need to waste time in trying to understand how it comes about. Accept it as a fact. Give serious consideration to its implications, and when you have recognised it as truth you will realise how important it is to discipline your destructive emotions and control your bad thoughts.

As a general rule, a generous person has well-formed lips while mean-mindedness and cruelty are associated with a thin tight mouth. Sharpened features usually go with acidity of temper, a tendency to suspicion or a life-denying asceticism. The fuller face denotes jollity, a philosophic outlook and a Yes-to-life attitude which in some cases may be a sign of an over-indulgence of the appetites. Facial development does not always conform to a set pattern but sooner or later the truth comes out in your face: what you are, what you think and how you think. Various forms of facial disguises and the ability to act may carry you through under a false mask for a few years but there is a limit to the extent to which time and truth can be cheated.

This, then, brings you back to the basic theme of this book: the acceptance of the fact that you have within you the power to direct the creative forces which affect not only your life but your physical appearance.

As thoughts are wayward, running this way and that like sheep without a shepherd, it follows that if you wish to encourage this power to work in your favour you must learn how to use it.

Make it a daily practice to inculcate into your mind the qualities which you most wish to see expressed in your character. Sit quietly for a few moments and think about kindliness, charitableness, forgiveness, love, peace. Let these words seep right down into your subconscious and feel their meanings. Use imagination to picture yourself as being already in possession of these virtues. Enact an imaginary scene in your mind in which you are being misjudged, criticised or ill-used in some way and see yourself as reacting, not vindictively, but kindly and courteously. Keep on projecting this new image of yourself onto the screen of your mind. In your imagination be the sort of person you desire to be and see yourself as you would like to appear in the eyes of others. If you do this often enough you will find that you will react in that way in real life when the circumstances arise, because you will have become used to this kind of reaction. Constant repetition has demonstrated the potency of the spoken word and the projected image. The person pictured on the photographic screen of the imagination has become the flesh-and-blood you. Where lies the dividing line between imagination and reality? Possibly there isn't one. Perhaps the varying stages of your mental and spiritual development unwind like a continuous filmstrip.

There will be many occasions when you will let yourself down badly. Off your guard you will come out with a pert retort to something which you considered to be unjust or offensive. Over-sensitive to criticism you will take a plunge back into the bad old habits of self-vindication and self-justification. Hurt by something done or said you will find yourself hitting out and hitting back. But do not be too shattered by these setbacks. If you are aiming at perfection you are playing for high stakes and you cannot afford to go to pieces every time you slip up. Keep at it. Keep on projecting the image of your ideal self-superimposed upon the erring stupid self that so often comes to the surface. Learn to forgive yourself and try again.

Do not limit your training to the morning and evening sessions that you devote to your private affirmations. Be at it all day. Wherever you are you can be practising. Life never stops. All through the day at home or at work you will be given opportunities of putting what you know into practice. Impose the rule of law upon the unruly rabble of thoughts that clamour for dominance. When a thought of rancour or resentment presents itself fling it out. Dismiss everything that is destructive or discordant. Replace it with thoughts of harmony. Meet agitation with serenity, cynicism with faith, fear with confidence, weakness with strength.

Be master in your own mental household. Every victory over yourself will make the next fight easier to win. Remember that as you make your character so you make your face. But the fruits of success have to be won over and over again if they are to be retained. There is no such thing as a static state. You are gaining ground or losing ground all the time. You can never stand still because the demons that are out to destroy you never let up for a moment. Constant vigilance is the price of perfection; so you can never be off your guard in the running battle of life. Time and time again you will have to cross the same bridges and fight over the same old ground so never congratulate yourself on a victory. Complacency is the forerunner of defeat. No wonder the Lord said, 'Pray without ceasing'.

The first moment at the beginning of the day is the best time for fixing your face by getting into the right attitude of mind. When you wake you bring with you something of the freshness of the supernatural world into which you have been withdrawn during sleep. You have been recharged with physical energy and your mind is still partially in touch with the realms of inspiration from which it has returned, so this is the moment for setting your sails in the right direction. Turn yourself in thought towards what is bright, good and beautiful. Pray that your own special guardian angel be with you whatever you do and wherever you go. This will send fears and forebodings scuttling away into the shadows. Resolve that you will do your best and look your best. Expect wonderful things to happen as you set out into the new day that God has given you, but before you present yourself to the world take a look in the mirror to make sure that the corners of your lips are arranged ready to lift into a smile at the first opportunity.

So much for the mental attitude. But there is another and more subtle factor to be considered in the making of a face namely the spiritual, and this, ultimately, is of more importance than the psychological. It is acknowledged that thought forces mould contours and that worry scores lines on the forehead, but the action of what is spiritual is less easy to define. It is expressed by the glow of the eyes, that inner light that shines with a joy that cannot be simulated. The eyes are the windows of the soul. Although the aura that surrounds you can be seen only by the psychic medium, it can be felt and sensed by those who have no psychic sensitivity. When an unhappy person enters a room the psychic temperature is lowered and the gloom surrounding that person is communicated to others. The opposite is true when you meet someone who radiates positive thoughts of happiness and health. No word may be spoken but you are influenced by the vibrations generated from within.

B

The beauty that comes from an inward peace has a luminous quality about it. It cannot be blighted by the passing of time, nor ravaged by sorrow. Through the life of the spirit your secret self becomes your public self because you cannot hide what you truly are. The health of your soul is apparent in your face. So are its weaknesses and its poverty.

The making of a new face is dependent upon your ability to think new thoughts. Never let your mind grow old and lazy. It needs to be kept supple by exercises in the same way as the body. If a limb is not used it becomes flabby and useless. So does a brain. Too many people are content to think the same old thoughts day after day, year after year, deadening little thoughts concerning food, entertainment, social and domestic trivialities. All these things have their places but they should never be allowed to occupy the mind to the exclusion of higher concerns. The soul has its claims and a mind that is always conscious of these claims will never lapse into senility.

Renewal is one of the fundamental laws of nature; the secret of renewal is the secret of perennial youth, so if you want to make a new face for yourself there is no time to be lost, for you are making it and remaking it with every thought you think. Emerson quotes St Bernard as saying, 'Nothing can work me damage except myself; the harm that I sustain I carry about with me, and never am a real sufferer but by my own fault.'

You do indeed carry about with you the harm done to your body and your face as a result of wrong habits of thinking. This cannot be put right by a single word or a single thought. Only by constant repetition of what is creative and regenerative can the mind build up the forces that can repair the damage. The longer you delay the harder it will be to change the negative into the positive, the destructive into the constructive, the old into the new.

Remember that minute by minute through the creative power of habitual thought you are making your life, making your soul and making your face.

[4]

PEACE AND POISE

The peace of the mind and the poise of the body are closely associated. If you are truly at peace within yourself it will be reflected in posture and movement, but if you live in a state of nervous agitation you will be restless and jerky. The poise that comes from an inner confidence in yourself is more than a matter of the carriage of the head and the set of the shoulders. Although right thinking is a factor in preventing the ills and ailments which stem from incorrect posture, the kind of poise that nothing can shake is not a self-conscious attitude, it is one of the many manifestations of spiritual equilibrium.

To achieve poise you must find peace, but it must be a peace that is creative and dynamic. The peace that is a mere cessation of mental and physical activity is not the kind of peace that will build you up and enrich your inner resources. To sit passively in a state of vacuous bliss will not get you very far. 'The peace that passeth all understanding' is not confined to the monastic cell or to the solitary meditations of the mystic, but can be found at the very heart of the hubbub of life. If you cannot find it there you will never be able to find it anywhere.

Where there is continual strife in a home or an industry the cross-currents of thought create the stormy conditions which generate friction. The atmosphere becomes charged with the explosive mental conditions which can be felt by those who are sensitive. Strife is destructive.

'In quietness and in confidence shall be your strength.' Those words were written nearly two thousand eight hundred years ago but how true they still are today! Confidence in what? Confidence in the great power into which your subconscious mind opens and to which you have immediate access. The underlying peace of this supreme power will sustain you through all the emergencies of life if you turn to it in trust.

'My peace I leave with you,' said the Master to the disciples as He sat at supper with them for the last time before walking out into the night to be tried and crucified. Did that mean that they were to enjoy a quiet life of contemplative piety? Certainly not. They were going to have to get out into the world and start a revolution that was destined to overturn, not only the Roman empire, but the whole conception of life for men everywhere. They were to be persecuted, flogged, ridiculed and martyred. And yet Jesus could sit there in that upper room and say, 'Peace I leave with you, my peace I give unto you: not as the world giveth, give I unto you. Let not your heart be troubled, neither let it be afraid.' He knew they would need the kind of peace that only He could give.

We all need that peace and the poise which comes from possessing it, but it does not drop out of heaven

like dew. It has to be sought. You will have to give up
a certain amount of time to the finding of it if you are
to possess it for your own. But it is worth every effort
that you can make. It is your strength. It is the pearl
of great price.

If there is something on your conscience you will
never be able to enjoy the full realisation of the peace
that is your strength. First clear the decks for action.
'First be reconciled to thy brother, and then come and
offer thy gift', said our Lord in the sermon on the
mountain. First the reconciliation. Then open your
mind to the inflowing of the peace that is your confidence and your strength.

Be a peace-maker and not a peace-breaker. Think
peace and live it. When important matters are being
discussed or when you have to give a decision pause
before speaking and direct your thoughts in the direction of peace. Say nothing that will deepen a rift or
make more trouble. 'Resist not evil, but overcome evil
with good.' That is one of the secrets of maintaining
peace not only in your life but in your body. Whatever
benefits your mind benefits your health so intimately
do mind and body interact.

Through your daily affirmations you can place yourself in a state of receptivity and receive into yourself
the transforming power of infinite peace. Until you
can do this you will never be a fully integrated personality, for you will be less than you might be, something
inferior to your ideal self.

As you progress in knowledge and experience of
practical psychology you will find gradually that the

subconscious mind will take over to the extent to which you have trained it to react along certain lines. If it has become permeated with life-giving, health-promoting and peace-making ideas it will react accordingly. If, for instance, you are provoked, you will not have to wait while you instruct your subconscious mind how it must react; the response will be almost automatic. Immediately a peaceful solution will be handed up to the objective mind as a good secretary will produce required information without waiting to be asked. The conciliatory thought will be flashed to the brain and the right word spring to the lips. But you can rely on this sort of reaction only if your subconscious has been thoroughly briefed. You cannot expect it to help you out of your difficulties if it has never been told what to do.

It all comes back to training. It is the daily repetition that lays the thought tracks of habit. Keep on telling yourself that you are at peace with the world. At every opportunity assert that there is this power of peace within you which is able to carry you quietly through situations of great difficulty, a power that can dispel animosity and turn discord into harmony. Thought is potent. You cannot see it and yet you can feel the working of its power to please or to antagonise, to hurt or to heal. When once you have demonstrated the power of a peaceful word you will be surprised to see how the magic chemistry works. Without a word being spoken it is possible to save an ugly situation simply with a smile or a kindly silence.

Composure is confidence, but remember that it is

not the unruffled self-satisfaction of the surface mind that can work the miracle of reconciliation with others, it is the peace that comes from deeper sources. This is the peace that keeps you poised so that instead of being blown this way and that with every wind that passes you are held in a state of psychic equilibrium, alert and yet relaxed.

If your thoughts get out of control and you are always hurrying forward mentally you will be inclined to thrust your head forward as you walk. This is because you are constantly telling yourself that you are busy and in a hurry and your body catches on to the idea and obeys blindly. It is trying to keep pace with your thoughts. You must beware of the temptation to press on with the next thing you have in mind before you have completed your present task. This is not easy to do in these days when the speed of life has been accelerated to the point of breakneck. People do not work so hard as they did in the old days but they cover more ground rushing to and fro along the roads or in the air. With more money to spend and more leisure in which to spend it they tend to move their bodies from one place to another at a greater speed, but this does not mean that they are being more useful or that they are enjoying themselves. They have merely been caught up in the feverish race of modern living. The treadmills turn faster and faster but they are still treadmills. Only those who have the desire and the courage to jump off know what it is to see the whole thing for the farce that it is.

'Stand still and consider the wondrous works of

God.' Old Job knew nothing about fast cars and jet aircraft but he knew about something better. He knew that if you want to see what life really amounts to you have to stand still and consider. So slow down the tempo wherever possible. Never be hurried or flurried. Tell yourself that there is more time than you think. Know that in reality there is no such thing as time at all. Clock and calendar time is meaningless in itself. These human reckonings are based upon the orderly movements of the heavenly bodies. Rest your busy mind on the eternal and not on what is temporal. This resting will relax you and help you to acquire poise. As you learn to rest more and more in the peace of timelessness you will begin to lose the habit of thrusting your head forward to get in front of your feet, a habit which leads to stooping shoulders and an unnatural stretching of the neck.

The body takes its cue from the mind. If you go round looking as if you had all the cares of the world upon your shoulders the spine will begin to sag under the weight of its imaginary burden. Old people tend to grow shorter because they grow into themselves, unable through habit to stand erect. Mind helps body and body helps mind, so stand straight and walk tall. When the head is lifted high in hope and confidence there is a corresponding lifting of the spirit and a quickening of the step as mind, soul and body co-operate.

Feet have as much to do with poise as the head, the shoulders and the mental outlook, so be merciful to your feet. Do not crush them into ill-fitting shoes.

Remember how well they have served you. Even if you walk no more than six miles a day your feet have to cover more than two thousand miles in a year. Walk carefully and well. Do not shuffle or scurry. A sprained ankle can give you a limp that will upset the whole balance of the body. Be grateful to your feet and give them plenty to do. If the distance is within your range, never drive or ride when you can walk. And when you sit, sit comfortably but gracefully. Do not sprawl or flop. Remember that your body is incorrigibly lazy. When you are tired or unwell it wants to slump. Do not encourage it to indulge in this kind of behaviour. The body, like the mind, must be trained.

Fear shrinks you. Courage stretches you to your full moral and mental stature, so live courageously. Face every morning in the spirit of adventure. Welcome everything that comes at you in the course of the day. If it is something good enjoy it and be grateful. If it is bad do not let it get you down. Know that there is a power at work in your life that can change water into wine and evil into good. Weigh the hardship and the happiness and you will find that the blessings outweigh the burdens. When you have mastered the art of weighing things up in this way you will find that you cease to become upset by passing troubles because you will have acquired that mysterious thing called poise.

Poise is the hallmark of the integrated character. One whose mind is all over the place and who lives on a see-saw of emotional crises can never gather himself up into a semblance of wholeness. Start now on the re-education of your mind, the conscious and the sub-conscious, in this matter of peace and poise. It is never too early or too late to begin.

YOUR IDEAL SELF

Within you potentially there is an ideal self, you as you would like to be, a self which embodies all the qualities that you most admire in other people. If you are honest with yourself you know your own weaknesses. You know the points at which you fall below the standard of that ideal self within you, but if you believe that it does lie latent underneath all the faults and failings you will gradually bring it into being. Every time you conquer a fault or wrestle successfully against wrong feelings you are assisting at the birth of your ideal self. Never lose hope or sight of the fact that it is there within you as the oak tree lies potential in the acorn. It is there; all that you might be, all that you wish to be, is waiting to be developed and perfected.

The transforming of the ideal into the real need not be a lengthy process, although it may be a painful one. But nothing worth having is cheap. The greater the value of the thing desired the more it will cost you in terms of time and trouble. You will have your disappointments as you find yourself reacting to something along the old thought tracks of bad habits, but you can make an instant recovery. The power to create a new self out of an old self is something that is almost magical, like the transformation of Cinderella's pumpkin into a golden coach.

Does this sound fantastic? Is it too good to be true? Consider some of the loveliest things in Nature: sunsets, stars, trees, dewdrops, snowflakes, birds and flowers. There is a touch of fantasy in all expressions of beauty. You are surrounded with beauty that cannot be explained in scientific or technological terms, so why boggle at this? Accept now the truth that you have the power within you to be better than you are, as healthy and as happy as you hope to be.

Perhaps you despair when you take a long cool look at what you are. You are all mixed up. You want to be happy, successful, efficient and good, but you do not know how to go about it. The old habits of thought are so strong. You give way to impatience, irritation, self-love, resentment, jealousy and all the other weaknesses Satan has in his bag of tricks to defeat and destroy you.

Remember that you were made in the image and likeness of God. Live up to what that means. Consider its implications. Think and act on the assumption that it is true. Waste no time in asking useless questions as to if and how. That is not your province. Your part of the work of bringing your ideal self into actuality is to believe in its possibility and to think and act on the basis of that belief. This may mean a certain amount of psycho-analysis, but you do not need a professional psychiatrist for this. You can do it yourself. Never let a day go by without a few moments of self-examination. There is always something to be put right, something you regret saying or doing. Admit the fault and erase the memory of it with a positive resolve to do better. Do not dwell on it. There is no need to take too seriously every detail that comes under the microscope of self-criticism. That only tends to make you self-conscious and introspective. You want to get away from the self as soon as you have acknowledged your error. Too much analysis bogs you down in the limitations of the objective mind. After you have confessed your sin and done your penance you need to make contact with the wider world that lies below and around the surface mind.

Affirm that you are what you wish to be. If you have been unkind, affirm that there is a power within you that is infinite love. If you have become involved in a quarrel, affirm that there is a power within you that is infinite peace. If you have been feeling unwell, affirm that there is a power within you that is infinite life. Switch from the negative to the positive as soon as you have put right what was wrong.

A practical method of helping to bring the ideal self into being is to take pencil and paper and make a list of all the qualities you feel you lack and would like to possess such as self-control, humour, patience, serenity, courage, forbearance. You yourself will know what virtues you need to cultivate, and concentrate on one thing for five or ten minutes three times a day if possible, if not make sure of doing this mental exercise at least morning and evening. And let your last thought at night be in the direction of what you desire to become in your ideal self, because a positively expressed desire works powerfully upon the subconscious when you are asleep and the objective mind is off duty.

In making your affirmations it is best to be alone, but there are often times in the day when even in the company of others it is possible to repeat silently one of the great life-affirming words. This wonderful work of creation and re-creation can go on when the hands are busy at a task or when the objective mind is working mechanically. Snatch every opportunity that presents itself. Fill every mental gap with something that is going to help bring about the realisation of what is desirable and ideal.

Every word or thought that puts an emphasis on what is unhealthy or unhappy will tear down what you are trying to build up, so watch your thoughts at every step. Life is full of traps and pitfalls. The higher you aim the more you will be subjected to temptation. Do not imagine that the devil is going to stand idly by while you change yourself trying to live God's way instead of his way. And do not delude yourself into thinking that there is no such entity as evil personified. Our Lord believed in the devil so it ill becomes you to adopt a superior attitude and dismiss him as a myth. If only he were! How easy life would be if we were never turned from our purposes by evil forces, but then we should never have to put up a fight. The will would grow flabby from lack of use. If you allow your mind to become a vacuum it will be wide open to the intrusion of marauding spirits whose delight it is to work mischief amongst the children of God.

Whenever this kind of spiritual crisis is experienced get back to your centre. Affirm the all-powerfulness of the Divine being who loves you and wants you to be your best self at all times reflecting His image.

Renew your mental picture of the ideal self within. Imagine yourself as you would wish to be: youthful in mind and body, alive and alert, radiating a spirit of cheerfulness, courage and loving kindness towards all. When the picture slips make the necessary adjustments. Establish the right image of yourself firmly in the mind, and never doubt that you are capable of becoming like this mental picture of your ideal self.

There will be times when you will despair of ever seeing your dream fulfilled in reality but keep at it and you will dream true. However often you blunder on from one mistake to another never let yourself go or let yourself down. Withdraw into the silence to re-charge the batteries and to recapture your dream.

If you have been unjust to somebody put it right on the personal level if that is possible, but if it is too late to make amends put it right mentally. Think only thoughts of love towards the person you have wronged or misjudged and in time those feelings of guilt will cease to torment you. And if you are the one who has been badly treated let your ideal self come uppermost. Do not react resentfully or vindictively. Do the difficult thing and let love take over, for love is a solvent that melts away the incrustations of grievances which can do untold harm if left to harden.

If your conscience tells you that you have been touchy, uncharitable or unreasonable throw it all into the melting pot of the silence and let God calm you down. The more you educate your subconscious mind to reject the negative and cultivate the positive the sooner you will be released from the tensions which give rise to discordant and unhappy situations.

Your ideal self must be trained to function harmoniously on the physical, the mental and the spiritual plane, and every part of the three-stranded cord of your personality must be kept in good order for it is as strong as its weakest link.

No affirmation of good is ever wasted. Even if you are suffering from some physical affliction for which there seems no immediate cure it cannot do anything but good to affirm the reality of health. In ways too subtle to define thought has a therapeutic effect upon nerves and tissues, so whatever the bodily condition may be never cease to hold before your inward gaze the constant image of your ideal self, the self that you wish to present to the world. Progress towards the fulfilment of desire will be determined by your powers of perseverance.

'Be ye transformed by the renewing of your mind', said Paul, and that is exactly what you are doing when you embark upon a course in practical psychology. Paul knew what so many now are coming to recognise, that you cannot change a sick man into a healthy man by prescribing drugs, nor can you change a bad man into a good man by preaching at him. The cure must come from within. The ideal can become the real only through the wonder-working Christ power that lies within. This alone can bring about the true transformation.

[6]

BALANCE AND RHYTHM

There is much in Yogism that is worthy of your consideration if you want to learn to practise a system of control over mind and body. Deep methodical breathing has a calming effect upon the nerves, and concentrating quietly upon a particular object does help to bring your wandering thoughts to a point of rest, but it must be remembered that the truths enshrined in the Christian's Bible are older than Yoga. The words 'Acquaint now thyself with Him and be at peace' were written over a thousand years before the Buddha was born. We can learn much from Hindu philosophy in these days of restlessness. Anything that makes you sit down and think quietly about something bigger than yourself is a good thing, but the best of its teaching is all there in the religions of the West.

The aims of life should be based on something more than the mere realisation of Nirvana. To deny the world is a negation of life because it is God's world and we have to live in it. The whole business of achieving unity through contemplation of the Divine was put into the singing mouth of David when he said, 'Be still and know that I am God'.

To be still is to be balanced. Physically you must have your body under control and mentally you must be in command with all the warring elements of the mind at rest.

Balance is harmony. We speak of the balance of Nature without realising what a marvellous thing it is. It is not visible to the eye but underneath all the complicated organisation there is a wonderfully worked out system of balance which has taken thousands of years to perfect. Man is destroying this balance and the destruction of it will in turn destroy him.

As in Nature so in life. There must be a point of equilibrium at which everything is held in a fine and beautiful state of balance.

Too much materialism brings the scale down heavily on one side, but religion adjusts the balance. An act of worship makes for humility and this serves to steady the balance against an overweight of pride and intellectual arrogance. The habit of prayer helps to keep you from making too much of yourself because it shifts the emphasis from the material to the spiritual, thus helping to maintain balance.

Balance is a very important factor on every plane of existence. We speak of a balanced diet, a balanced outlook, an unbalanced mind, a balancing of accounts, the balance of the body. Balance is a natural thing, something that is built into the mechanism of creation, but it cannot be properly maintained without control. To keep your balance in life amidst the chances and changes of circumstances you must be able to control your thoughts, your words, your actions and your emotions. Practise controlling yourself before you attempt to control others.

When you have mastered the science of balance you have gone a long way towards mastering the science of living, which is the understanding of how to attain and maintain a delicate balance between tension and relaxation, dreaming and doing, working and resting, the poise and counterpoise of the secular and the sacred. In simpler terms, how to combine the ideal and the practical.

The anatomy of the human body is a far more complicated and fantastic piece of machinery than a space rocket or a Jumbo jet but we tend to take it all for granted because it is self-regulating. It can keep on ticking over for eighty years without maintenance. A little food and a little liquid are all it needs for efficient working. You are a walking miracle. A glance at a diagram of the human frame is like looking at the inventor's design of some wonderful machine with its intricate arrangement of nerves, muscles, bones and glands. You can see it all on the diagram but some of the most amazing aspects of the body's life cannot be illustrated on paper. You cannot draw a diagram of this marvellous thing we call balance. You know that it has something to do with the ear and the brain but that does not help you to understand what it is.

When you look at a ballet dancer balancing the whole weight of the body on the tips of the toes, standing still, swaying, leaping, you are seeing a demonstration of unconscious control. The movements of the dancer are initiated by the brain, but in order to obey the dictates of the brain she must have a blind faith in the ability of the body to carry out the directions. So unquestioningly does she trust the body to be able to balance itself that she does not even think about it.

What keeps you upright? Why do you not fall over when you step out of bed in the morning? How is it that you are able to control your spine when you are running for a bus or stooping to pick something up? It is a good thing to ask yourself this sort of question occasionally. It develops an awareness of the mystery of creation. The working of a mechanical invention is described in the specification which accompanies the application for a patent, but no such specific explanation as to how your body maintains and reconditions itself can be found in a medical textbook. You know that it happens but you cannot say why it happens without acknowledging the existence of a supreme intelligence. Blind evolutionary forces could never have produced the miracle of your physical body.

Another aspect of the mystery of life is rhythm. In Nature you have the rhythmic coming and going of the seasons, sleeping and waking, light and dark, sunrise and sunset, growth and decay, the ebbing and the flowing of tides. The body too has its rhythms. Left right, left right go the feet. You cannot walk properly without keeping to the balance of rhythm. In and out goes the breath. Beat, beat goes the heart. Tick, tick goes the pulse. Not only are you a walking miracle but you are a piece of living music because so many of your vital organs work to the poetry of rhythm.

Your very life depends upon the inhaling and exhaling of breath. The filling and the emptying of your lungs goes on automatically. All you have to do is to breathe. But how do you breathe?

There is a way in which the natural act of breathing can serve as a means of helping you in the development of your ideal self thus, incidentally, affecting your life at every level of expression. It is what the Yogis call dynamic breathing.

First thing in the morning, and whenever you are able to make time for it, stand before an open door or window and take a deep breath, inhaling and exhaling to a slow and conscious rhythm. This not only exercises half used lungs, but it establishes rhythm and you can synchronise this rhythm with the repetition of your affirmations of health.

Know that when you breathe you are breathing in something more than oxygen. You are taking into yourself an element which is able to stimulate the mind, feed the soul and strengthen the body. The Yogis call this element, *prana*. It is what passed into the nostrils of Adam in the story of the second creation. In the first chapter of Genesis we read, 'So God created man in his own image, in the image of God created he him; male and female created he them.' This was the first creation: man as a physical being given dominion over everything that moved upon the earth. The story of the second creation comes in the following chapter. It may be that millions of years elapsed between the two stages, for who can measure in terms of time the length of a day in the mind of the Creator? And when all was made ready, when the earth had been planted and watered and the Lord had had his rest, the stage was set for the advent of man as a spiritual being. And so we have the story of the second creation: 'And the Lord God formed man of the dust of the ground, and breathed into his nostrils the breath of life; and man became a living soul.' From this moment Adam became something more than a man of the earth earthy. He became a living soul. But this great leap forward up the scale of development could not have taken place through any process of blind biological evolution. Adam became a living soul only when the breath of life was breathed into him by God.

You cannot grow to your full moral and spiritual stature unless you have been re-created by this mysterious thing called the breath of life. Jesus might have had the story of the two creations in mind when He said, 'Ye must be born again'.

Use your marvellous respiratory apparatus in the service of practical psychology and devote a regular period of time each day to the conscious act of breathing *prana* into your lungs. You will be taking into yourself an element more rarefied than air, the subtle life-giving element that is essential to your bodily, mental and spiritual well-being.

Know what you are doing when you practise dynamic breathing. Realise that you are inhaling life itself. Not only is the rhythmic inhalation of oxygen beneficial to the blood in its circulatory passage through the body, but the very act of repeating your affirmations of health in tune with the rhythm of the breath makes for harmony. As you breathe declare mentally or verbally that through the action of *prana* you are drawing new energy into your system. Tell yourself that fresh forces of vigour and rejuvenation are coursing through you and if you persevere you will be able to feel that this truly is what is happening. And when you expel the used air from your lungs do it methodically, in the same way realising the meaning of what you are doing. Remind yourself that you are expelling not only the carbon-dioxide but the fatigue, and all the poisonous waste-products of wrong thinking and wrong living. Let it all go. Breathe it out and pick up the rhythm again on the rising wave of a new breath.

As you become more experienced in your practice of dynamic breathing you will begin to look forward to it because it will act on you like a tonic that is both stimulating and relaxing. In time the mental part of it will become more and more like a form of praying as you make your communion with the Life that sustains all life.

Choose carefully the words that you are going to use in your affirmation, for you are the only one who knows what you really want. If health is your chief concern tell yourself that you are breathing into your body the spirit that generates the power that creates healthy conditions. Develop your own personal method, but remember that the principle on which you are working is universal. When you have felt the bracing effect of dynamic breathing and experienced the new sense of vitality that comes to you as a result of habitual practice you will become aware of an inner release of tensions. The rhythm of dynamic breathing has a

soothing influence upon jangled nerves and the tendency to jerky movements.

By this one simple exercise you will come into a new
inheritance of health and happiness, for you will have
become practised in the art of balance and control.
By the natural process of breathing in and breathing
out you can make yourself into a new person, so do not
neglect to recognise the important part played by conscious rhythmic breathing in the reorientation of the
subconscious mind.

[7]

THE THERAPY OF HAPPINESS

The words pleasure and happiness are not synony-
mous although it would be hard to say where the
different meanings overlap. Pleasure can be found in
the enjoyment of material things but there is a will-o-
the-wisp quality about this kind of superficial happiness. It is elusive. It is often found where you would
least expect to find it and not to be found where you
were certain that it was going to be. And when you do
find happiness in this world you can never be sure that
it will be permanent. There is no guarantee that it will
last.

Joy is of a different nature for it is related to what
is eternal in man. Our Lord once said that He had
come that our joy might be full. How is it possible to
experience this kind of joy, the joy that springs from
the deeps, the joy that is not dependent upon outward
conditions or upon our relationships with other
people? What is this private heaven of the mystic?
Some feel it through music, poetry or other forms of
art. Others possess it in the beauties of Nature or
through some kind of religious experience, but from

whatever source it comes true joy is always therapeutic. It can do you more good physically than anything that can be prescribed by a doctor or bought at
a chemist's shop.

Solomon, one of the wisest men who ever lived, said
in one of his proverbs that 'a merry heart doeth good
like a medicine: but a broken spirit drieth the bones'.
So he knew all there was to know about the power of
the mind to exercise a good or a bad influence on the
health of the body. Merriment is medicinal. Hopeless-
ness dries the bones and produces arthritic or rheum-
atic conditions. It may not necessarily be your own
unhappy mental state which causes the trouble. You
can catch it from other people like catching a germ.
That is why it is vital to develop a defensive attitude
by building up around yourself a protective atmosphere of cheerfulness and optimism. Never anticipate
that the worst is going to happen. Expect only the best
and it will come to you.

Natural merriment is something that is rare in these
days of non-stop so-called entertainment on television
or radio. Many of the programmes inflicted on the
public are supposed to be funny but a real comedian
is a rare phenomenon now. Wit seems to have been
crushed under the dull weight of vulgarity, though the
instinct for laughter is still there. Occasionally one
hears an outburst of it from children, a natural bubbling up of spontaneous laughter. This comes very
near to pure joy. Laughter is good for the muscles of
the stomach. It is also good for one's mental outlook
on life. There is nothing like a good laugh for changing

the perspective and making you see things from a different angle.

Laughter is one of God's loveliest gifts to man. The ability to smile is a safety valve. If you can smile at misfortune you have got the better of it. Without a word being uttered you can establish good relations with another person by the mere lifting of the corners of the lips into a smile and when this happens the eyes have a way of brightening. The face becomes a mirror reflecting happiness and goodwill. When you look at creatures like frogs, peacocks, grasshoppers, zebras or ducks you cannot resist the conclusion that the Creator was not lacking in a sense of humour.

The process of mind training must include the re-capturing of the capacity to laugh and in order to do this we must rediscover our lost innocence. The trouble with the human race now is that it knows more than is good for it. It has been prying about amongst the secrets of the universe and adding to its store of knowledge without making any corresponding ad-vances in ethics. The burden of all this scientific know-ledge weighs heavily upon our minds. We have found out how to destroy not only ourselves but the sea, the air and the earth. No wonder we have forgotten how to be gay.

The people who have least in life seem to be those who get the most fun out of it. 'How hard it is for a rich man to enter the kingdom of heaven', said Jesus. Not because there is anything intrinsically evil in money itself but because it tempts a man to pay more attention to the non-essentials of materialism at the expense of what is essential to his true health and well-being. People who have too much money are usually so busy wondering how to spend it, what to invest in and how much is going to be left over when the tax gatherers have had their share that they have little time for living the sort of life that includes laughter.

A sense of humour has averted many a breakdown. Mental instability is often caused by worry and too much self-concern. If you are able to laugh at yourself you will be less likely to lose control of yourself and your circumstances. 'Count it all joy,' said St Paul and there you have a whole philosophy of life in four brief words.

If you have within you this joyousness of spirit that nothing can quench you will have come into possession of one of the greatest secrets in the living of the good and glorious life, for nothing will ever truly hurt you. Grief, sorrow, disappointment, misfortune. You will have to grapple with them all, for nobody escapes in a world where such things do happen. But underneath all your pains and problems there will be this sense of happiness. It is your soul trying to tell you that all is well because deep down you are in touch with the Eternal, which is joy everlasting.

Without this inner joy you will be a prey to bitterness. Anxiety will take its toll. Worry will fray your nerves. Depression will rob you of mental and physical vitality. In due course these negative states of mind will show out in the body in some form of disease or discomfort. Do not let this happen. Use the law of cause and effect so that it works for you towards harmony and health instead of against you, bringing ill-effects in its train. Make no mistake about it. The law operates for good or for evil. It is up to you to see that it works in your favour by opening your mind to the source of all joy. Let it pour through you. Give yourself up to it. Invite it into your thoughts and into your heart. Make a channel in your mind through which it can flow, like a flashing stream.

The inner joy is also an inner light for it has the power to radiate. We speak of a face glowing with happiness. When Moses came down from Sinai after talking with God 'the skin of his face shone; and they were afraid to come nigh him'; so bright was the radiance that he had to wear a veil. When Christ was transfigured on the mountain his face shone like the sun and his garments were 'white and glistering'. The same thing happened to Stephen, the first Christian martyr of whom it was said that his face became the face of an angel.

Robert Louis Stevenson in one of his greatest and loveliest poems speaks of the 'great task of happiness' as if it were our bounden duty not only to be happy but to look happy.

> If I have faltered more or less
> In my great task of happiness;
> If I have moved among my race
> And shown no glorious morning face;
> If beams from happy human eyes
> Have moved me not; if morning skies,

Books, and my food, and summer rain
Knocked on my sullen heart in vain:
Lord, thy most pointed pleasure take
And stab my spirit broad awake.

When reading those humbling words I never want
to go beyond that point to the concluding four lines.
To ask God to stab you wide awake if you have been
ill-tempered or ungrateful for the common blessings of
life is to ask a terrible thing. All too often it is easy to
remember instances which bring you before the bar of
this judgment. Sharp recollections of recent failures
probe at the exposed nerves of your conscience. You
weren't feeling too good that morning. You were in a
mad rush for the train. The post had brought in a disturbing letter; and too many bills. An item on the
news had brought your temper to boiling point. You
couldn't find your car keys. The weather was foul.
Everything seemed to be conspiring against you so
when you spoke you were not as kind as you might
have been. You took it out of the first person within
earshot. What should have been your 'glorious morning face' became a scowling mask. You forgot to be
gracious. Or in plain theological language, the devil
got into you.

One of the parrot-like criticisms levelled at the
churchgoer by the non-churchgoer is that religion is a
gloomy affair. Like most facile generalisations it may
contain a grain of truth, but those who perpetuate this
old fallacy, never having taken steps to prove the truth

of it, should look in at a Christian Science church when a service is being held. This is where to go if you want to see a living demonstration of the 'glorious morning face'. Here you find no social froth, no talk of fund raising, no fussy concern with non-religious matters, no chatter about ills and ailments in the porch for there are no porches and no acknowledged ailments. Here you see what Christians are like when they concentrate solely on putting into practice literally and absolutely the precepts and principles expounded in Galilee. As the congregation sits facing the reading desk it sees not saints in stained-glass windows but two inscriptions in plain lettering on bare walls, one from the New Testament and one from *Science and Health*, written by Mary Baker Eddy:

YE SHALL KNOW THE TRUTH AND THE
    TRUTH SHALL MAKE YOU FREE.

DIVINE LOVE ALWAYS HAS MET AND
    ALWAYS WILL MEET EVERY HUMAN
    NEED.

and at the entrance the warning words, SILENCE IS MAINTAINED.

Which of these three statements provides the key to the secret of all those radiant faces, those happy people exuding a spirit of health and peace? Perhaps it is a combination of all three gathered up into the one word—joy.

Churchgoers or non-churchgoers we are all engaged

c

in what Robert Louis Stevenson describes as 'my great task of happiness'. Perhaps we should achieve greater success in finding and expressing happiness if we did really look upon it as a task, something that has to be worked at with persistent effort. This brings you back to the daily training of the conscious and the sub-conscious mind. Look upon it as a sacred obligation to put up a show of happiness even if at first you are play-acting. The very effort of pretending will impress the idea of happiness upon the part of your mind which is susceptible to suggestion. You are what you think you are—so think happiness. Make a habit of it. Think it and will it. So fill your thoughts with health, happiness and harmony that there will be no room left for the entertainment of thoughts that tend towards defeatism or depression.

Continual worry is a blasphemy against the God of joy. Anxiety, pessimism, fearfulness and fretfulness are all sins of the mind which, if persisted in, will destroy you in the end· But this philosophy of living must not be interpreted solely as a means of self-preservation or as a withdrawal from the hard realities of life. You have to decide which is real, the good or the bad. In trying to live joyously you are not only benefiting yourself but those with whom you have to live and work. You cannot change a situation by worrying over it, but you can change it by praying over it. It is for you to decide which method of tackling your problem you are going to adopt: the destructive and the futile or the constructive and the practical.

As you set out for work at the beginning of the day

remember that you have two jobs in hand. Not only must you do your best at the job for which you are paid, but you must also make a success of your great task of happiness. So before setting out for the day take a look in the mirror and check on your 'glorious morning face'.

8

FULLY STRETCHED

Lord Reith, on whose integrity and imagination the BBC built up the high standards of efficiency and good taste for which it was once famous, spoke in a television interview of being fully stretched.

To be fully stretched is to live in such a way that your mental, spiritual and physical powers are in constant use. It is all too easy to allow yourself to go slack. If your thoughts are working all the time round and round in the same old circle it means that there are parts of the brain that are never brought into use. The imagination becomes feeble, not having anything to do, and seldom stretched. If you shut yourself away from the problems and perplexities of an active life your mind will be deprived of exercise. In time it will become lazy and unwilling to make an effort.

Keep your mind in training. Give it something to work on. Do not be content to sit night after night before a television screen passively absorbing ideas, good and bad, in a state of negative mesmerism. Set yourself a mathematical problem. Memorise a poem. Read a stimulating book. Learn a language, or an instrument. Study. Write. Engage in an interesting discussion on some worthwhile subject. Go to a lecture or play a game of cards. Do something to stretch your mind beyond the limits imposed by habit and routine. Never say you are too old to bother. The mind does not age, it only seems to do so through not being used to its fullest extent.

Like everything else the mind needs to be renewed from time to time. Do not be satisfied with what you are. Set off on a new thought track and see what you can find. And do not be content with being your usual conventional self. Several different individuals lie potential within you so let them all evolve. Develop every gift you possess. Live more than one life at a time. For most people the bread-and-butter job takes only eight hours of the day. That leaves another sixteen in which to eat and sleep. What do you do with those sixteen hours? If you allow seven for sleep and one for travelling you are still left with eight. Resolve now to stretch your mind into a new dimension, even if it is only on the practical level of a useful hobby like carpentry, decorating or gardening. You do not know what you are capable of until you try. You will surprise yourself when you see what you can be and what you can do.

The body also needs to be stretched. Neglect of stretching the limbs leads to some of our present-day infirmities. Many people sit all day in an office and most of the evening at home. To go a journey of no more than a mile they will use the car. Legs need to be stretched and hearts need to be made to work.

Stretching is a natural movement. Watch a cat

waking from sleep and see how it stretches itself slowly and thoroughly. Do this every morning on waking but do it consciously, realising that as you stretch your limbs you are stimulating the flow of the life forces to the extremities. Visualise yourself as being filled with new life down to the toes and out to the fingertips. Never make a jerky movement. Keep it leisurely and graceful and enjoy it in an almost sensuous way. You will feel the benefit of this when you get out of bed and begin to walk about. Make a regular habit of this kind of stretching exercise and you will be less likely to suffer from the ailments which result from deposits in the joints.

Some areas of the body are sadly neglected in the matter of exercise. Do not forget your neck. Stretch it. And as you stretch the neck you lift the head. This in turn helps to square the shoulders and straighten the spine.

Five minutes stretching at the beginning of every day will keep you supple. It will do you more good than ten minutes of vigorous exercises. Not only will this improve the condition of the muscles but you will find that a series of slow, gentle stretchings will also have a beneficial effect upon internal organs, for the body is a whole. It does not consist of separate and unrelated parts. It is a unity and every healthy cell makes its own contribution to the general health of the whole body.

Because you are a trinity of soul, body and mind you must not forget that the soul, too, is in constant need of a good stretch. It doesn't get the exercise it re-

quires for its health. Some souls, alas, get none at all
and so they become deformed and stunted in their
growth. The unknown author of the great mystical
work called *The Cloud of Unknowing* speaks of man's
desire for God as a 'blind stretching' and that in a
sense is what prayer is: a blind stretching of the soul
towards what is holy and a straining away from what
is worldly and material. It is a reaching up to heaven,
its true home, for it knows that here it is a stranger
with no abiding place.

Every time you pray you stretch yourself spiritually.
Every time you sacrifice yourself and your own interests for the good of another you are stretching the stiff
limbs of the soul into activity. Every time you lose
yourself in the contemplation of beauty you are exercising the supernatural part of your threefold being,
the part of you that reaches out into realities that lie
beyond the reach of the intellect. Every act of dis-
interested love is an extending of yourself into a higher
dimension than that upon which you exist in the give
and take of daily living. Such love stretches you beyond
the measure of your ordinary self.

But how often does this happen? Is it not true that
spiritually speaking we are only half alive? We have a
tight little moral code that keeps us out of mischief,
more or less; a neat ethical creed that satisfies the conscience and enables us to see ourselves as reasonably
law-abiding according to the conventional idea of
righteousness, but it is not enough for a soul that wants
to come alive with the new kind of life envisaged by
Christ. A soul that never has a chance of expressing

itself develops cramp, shut up in the small cage of an unspiritual religion when it wants to expand and explore as a bird stretches its wings for flight.

Take time to consider this neglected aspect of your three-level existence here on earth. The physical part of yourself that has a name and a face is what other people see, but the part of you that can be seen only by the eye of God is the real you, the naked you with all your faults, your failings and your pretensions; it is the only part of you that will survive the change called death. And yet how badly you treat your real self, cramping its growth and starving it to the point of extinction.

When you have realised the truth that health is wholeness and that to enjoy perfect health you must be well in every part of your mental, physical and spiritual being you will understand the necessity of the stretching process.

Your body with its limbs, your mind with its thoughts and your spirit with its yearnings, are all dependent for their health upon keeping a right balance between tension and relaxation. But as we all tend to be indolent, however busy we may appear to be on the surface, it is necessary to make a conscious effort to maintain this rhythm of contraction and stretching, drawing in and reaching out.

When you meditate in the silence you are in a state of apparent rest; your intellectual faculties are quiescent, your body is still, hands folded, limbs and nerves held in a state of quietness, but your soul, the real you, is being stretched. With the objective mind temporarily out of action because under control, the soul becomes aware of itself. As if by a magnetic compulsion it turns itself towards God and in so doing it is refreshed and strengthened. When it has stretched itself before the face of God and warmed itself in the sunshine of the Divine presence it is able to convey to the body and to the mind something of what it has experienced. To the body it comes as a new influx of vitality; to the mind it comes as a stimulation of its creative powers.

The reorientating of the subconscious mind towards the realities of health, happiness and harmony is dependent upon your ability to stretch yourself fully on every plane of your existence as a mental, physical and spiritual being. This is what you are doing when you make your daily affirmations.

9

THE ARCHIVES OF MEMORY

If your memory failed you would not be able to function as a responsible person, for you are your memory. A complete breakdown of this faculty would mean that you would be unable to remember your name or address. You would be lost to life.

The memory can be likened to a records office where everything is filed away for future reference. How often you hear somebody say, 'My memory is terrible. I can't remember anything these days.' Never say it. Your memory is not terrible. It has become lazy through lack of exercise, so do not say untrue things about yourself. Remember that what you express in words takes shape in reality and becomes true; such is the power of the spoken word. Train yourself to voice only that which is positive and true.

Before analysing the workings of memory in relation to the subconscious mind pause for a moment to reflect upon what a marvellous thing it is, far more wonderful than the scientific equipment that gets a man to the moon or the computer that tells you how much money you have in the bank. There is a technological explanation for all man-made inventions, but no surgeon

74

has ever opened up somebody's brain and seen his memory.

Consider some of the amazing things that the memory can do. It can reach down into the subconscious mind and locate information you thought had been lost forever. Through memory you can relive past experiences. You can see the faces of the children with whom you went to school. You can recollect their names and recall things done and said that you have not thought about for thirty, forty or fifty years.

Memory is not the same thing as imagination. The imagination can make pictures for you to look at of people whom you have never seen and places you have never visited, but memory confines its operations only to that which is real—things, people, places and events recalled from actual experience. And memories, when evoked, have the power to create emotional responses of pleasure or unhappiness, which in their turn produce physical effects. The thought of some remembered grief in your life can suddenly squeeze a tear out of a dry eye. The recollection of a happiness can send a warm glow through your veins and the remembrance of something that once frightened you can chill you and cause you to shudder. So memory is not just a shadowy affair of calling up ghosts out of the past. It is a practical and cleverly contrived instrument for ensuring the continuity of thought, which holds the personality together and connects the past with the present. It is the working of the memory that keeps you ticking over mentally. The insane are insulated against the impact of the outside world, contained

within their immediate environment and the sensa-
tions of the present moment. Memory releases the
mind from this sort of imprisonment because it is the
memory that establishes your identity and keeps you
linked in a living relationship with other people.

Memory is not only a means of communication
between today and yesterday or this year and last
year. This is only one of its functions, and in order that
it should work for you in practical matters you must
train it in the way it should go. Think of it as a storehouse, for that is what it is. Within it lie the records
of all the ideas that have left an impression upon your
mind. In this storehouse things may sometimes be
mislaid, but they are never lost.

A memory that is not kept at full stretch is in danger
of becoming feeble and eventually useless, so give it
plenty to do. Train it by setting yourself every day
certain exercises for this purpose. Learning the lines of
a poem is a good idea for this kind of training because
the rhymes help with the mechanical side of remembering. Another helpful exercise is the repetition of
multiplication tables or the learning of Biblical texts
with chapter and verse.

If you want to make a success of this method of
memory training you must realise the importance of
concentration. Vague thoughts never get through.
They flutter away into the great wastepaper basket of
the inchoate and the inept. So when you are doing
this mental drill do it consciously. Pay attention to
what you are saying. Do not let half your mind go to
sleep. All kinds of distractions will try to drag your

thoughts away from the point of concentration but you must keep on bringing them back to the realisation of what you are doing. Talk to your memory and tell it what you want it to do. Whatever it is that you wish to remember, hold it in your mind for a moment before you let it drop down into the subconscious to be stored away in the archives of memory. You will not have to wait long for results. If you make the effort and keep at it regularly you will find within a week or so that your memory will become more reliable and your mind more alert. Your powers of concentration will have improved and this feeling of mental regeneration will produce a corresponding increase in your physical vigour.

One of the best assets you can have in business is the ability to remember facts, figures and faces in a flash. A memory that is working efficiently will respond immediately to any demands made upon it by the objective mind. It will be able to run straight down the thought tracks to the point at which the required information is stored away in the files of the subconscious. This information will then be transmitted to the right department. All this happens so quickly as to be instantaneous and almost automatic.

Many a mistake has been put right and many lives saved from the consequences of unwise decisions by the coming of an afterthought. Where do these afterthoughts come from, these thoughts that come up unbidden to rescue you from the results of folly and wrong thinking? Some time after a decision has been made and the matter forgotten you will have the un-

easy feeling that you should give it further consideration. Unknown to you the memory has been at work
in co-operation with the subconscious brought into
action by that great Power within you that wants to
protect and preserve you, that beneficent all-knowing
Power that is always working for your highest good.
But you cannot have an afterthought without a first
thought, and the two are connected by memory.

This brings us back to your reliance on the subjective part of your mind for all that you need for
successful living.

Learn to trust your memory, for you are dependent
upon it for keeping open the lines of communication
between all the various levels on which you function,
the objective, the subjective, the physical and the
spiritual. Memory feeds the subconscious and the subconscious feeds memory, the two act and interact to
serve your best interests if you will only give them the
right principles on which to go to work. This rests with
you. It is for you to decide whether you are going to
direct these powers towards success or failure, health
or disorder, prosperity or poverty.

Set aside regular periods during the day to the
proper direction of these wonder-working powers and
you will be astonished how quickly they will begin to
work for your betterment. Remember that you must
never put into words what you do not wish to see
materialised. So do not fall into the habit of saying
that you can't remember things. By impressing that
thought upon the subconscious you are making a
reality of it.

There is no reason why the memory should deteriorate with advancing years. A well-trained memory should last you a lifetime if habits of thinking, living and eating are controlled along the right lines.

The most rewarding method of memory training is to take pencil and paper and make a list of your blessings. One by one the various items will come crowding into your mind and when you think there are no more to be added your subconscious mind will produce another and another. Not only will this daily practice help to stretch the memory but the gratitude that comes with the remembering will leave its own dower of blessings in its train, for there is nothing like gratitude for lifting the heart and turning thoughts in the direction of what is life-giving and beneficial.

10

THE CURRENT THAT KNOWS ITS WAY

You will never be able to float until you are willing to trust the water. A lesson in floating is a lesson in confidence. Without questioning you have to accept the fact that the water can take your weight. As soon as you doubt it you go under. Peter found that out to his cost when he jumped over the side of his boat and tried to walk on the water as Jesus was doing. It was all right so long as he believed he could do it but when his nerve cracked down he went. The same principle applies in learning to trust the Supreme Power. You must abandon yourself to it in absolute faith knowing that 'underneath are the everlasting arms'.

If you have some dreaded interview before you or if you have to face up to any sort of unpleasant ordeal you must first cast out fear, then fling your whole weight upon the Power that is able to hold and sustain you under any circumstances.

Swedenborg said things that were so revolutionary in the field of philosophy, theology and metaphysics that the world has not yet got round to understanding what he was trying to say. He said, 'They that are in the stream of Providence are borne continually to happiness no matter what the appearance of the means', and Emerson, later, was in the same stream of thought when he spoke of 'the current that knows its way'. The same thought was expressed by Shakespeare: 'There's a divinity that shapes our ends.' If you would be carried towards your highest and greatest good you must trust the stream of Providence and cease to think of yourself as a piece of driftwood bobbing about on the restless and unpredictable sea of life. Know that you are in the flow of Divine blessing, 'the current that knows its way'.

This is not to say that you are relieved of the responsibility of exercising your will. You are free to choose whether you will give yourself up to the current that knows its way or strike off in some direction of your own, trusting entirely to the guidance of your own impulses.

Do not push against supernatural pressures. Emerson said that the soul's emphasis was always right. If you have to suffer as a consequence of your own mistakes do not go to pieces. Take your punishment and learn what it has to teach. When you are caught in the machinery of the law of cause and effect do not think of yourself as a helpless and unlucky victim. Renew your determination to work in co-operation with this immutable law and accept your experience as part of your unfolding development.

The main course of your life is traced out by an intelligence beyond your own. Some call it fate, some call it destiny and some call it God, but whatever name you give to this overruling power you must remember that you are always free to exercise your own will and to make your own decisions. That is why it is essential to acknowledge this supernatural and superconscious power. Recognise it at work in your life and the closer you live in communion with it the more sensitive you will be to its promptings.

You may wonder how you are to know whether you are being guided by providential will or by your own personal desires. How can you tell the difference between spiritual intuition and superficial impulse? Experience alone can teach you this. When things have gone hopelessly wrong for you look back to the beginning in a spirit of humility prepared to see and to admit where you made an unwise move.

Impulses must be kept on a tight rein. When you get an urge to do a certain thing make sure first that it springs from right motives. Bring the whole thing out into the daylight of Divine wisdom. Go to your Bible. Find a relevant passage and repeat it over and over in your mind. The truth of it will seep down into your subconscious mind and influence your feelings. If the idea persists after having been subjected to a higher judgment than your own it is usually safe to let it have its way.

Intuition is more reliable than impulse. Intuition is like a third eye with which you are able to see beyond the range of the physical. Your two eyes are marvellous enough. If in good condition they will be able to see for miles, but the third eye of the intuition is more wonderful still. It is an extra organ with which you can become aware of things that have no shape or colour.

It is not outsight, but insight. Through this extraordinary faculty you know things without being told. Not only do you see people but you see through them. Intuition is also a third ear. It is attuned to the vibrations which communicate knowledge without words. As you develop the power of intuition you will always know what to do and what to say, for without listening consciously you will get the message.

Learn to understand how Divine guidance can be interpreted through the language of circumstances. Develop this capacity of understanding and you will not be upset when things appear to go against you. If you are in difficulties do not admit defeat at the first setback, but if difficulties increase in spite of your perseverance stand back and take stock of the situation. Are you on the right course? Could it be that God is trying to tell you something by making everything go wrong?

Do not resist this sort of opposition. Stop pushing at a bolted door. Perhaps you are trying too hard. Let it rest for the time being and fall back on your trust in the omniscience of the power behind the changing kaleidoscope of events.

We think we know what we are doing and where we are going, but it often happens that we end up by doing something entirely different from what we had envisaged. Unknown to us at the time, we responded to the pressure of the unseen and without realising it we changed course and were carried along by a force that was gentle but irresistible.

So when things do not seem to be working out as

you hoped do not pull against the tide. Let go and let God take charge. Give up struggling. Many of life's troubles come about as a result of refusing to accept what is inevitable and unalterable. Cultivate mental flexibility. Be still and listen to what is being spelt out for you through the actions and reactions of other people.

Never think that you have been launched on the sea of life in a boat without a sail heading for nothingness. You have your own destiny to fulfil. Nobody else can fulfil it for you. Believe in this destiny. As you increase your faith and follow where it leads you will become conscious of an unseen hand on the helm. Without realising it at the moment that it happens you will find yourself being guided in a certain direction. As one by one these wonderful experiences come you will begin to realise that when you get into the right current you are then borne along towards your ultimate fulfilment. You expect great things of every day as it comes. You anticipate good. In all the big crises of daily living, like choosing your job, making friends, falling in love or deciding where to live, you have a sense of pre-destination. It is as if you were meant to meet a certain person, to read a particular book or to go to a certain place at a certain time. You were free and yet you did what you did and went where you went under a feeling of compulsion. Once you stop believing in the non-sensical idea of chance and start believing in the power that has a purpose to work out in and through you, life will take on a new look. You will set out each day wondering what fresh and lovely surprise life holds in store for you. You will begin to live in a world touched by magic, a world in which anything can happen.

Decide now to plunge in at the deep end. Do not be content with paddling around in the shallows. Trust yourself to the invisible arms even though at first it may look dark and dangerous out there. A strong current runs below the surface of the water, but it is a current that knows its way.

11

THE DOCTOR WITHIN

Before you take your aches and pains to the local G.P. remember that you have a doctor within you who is on duty night and day working to keep you fit. Give this doctor a chance now and again. Trust him. He wants to make you well and keep you well. If anything goes wrong he rushes immediately to the affected part to ward off the danger whether it comes in the form of a virus, a germ, a fracture, a cut or any other threat of disease or discomfort. He is the healing power of Nature within you, the power that puts up a resistance to everything that is detrimental to the health of your body. This is the power that knits together the two ends of a broken bone and the two edges of a wound. The surgeon makes the incision but the doctor within heals it.

For minor ailments the local practitioner can do nothing for you that you cannot do for yourself. Most minor ailments get better eventually whether you have treatment or not, so you are doing your doctor a service by not taking up time which he probably needs for patients in need of immediate attention.

One of the main evils of the National Health Service

is that you have to register with a doctor. This compels you to think of yourself as a potential patient, which is a bad thing. We should live in the daily expectation of good health, not ill health. The doctor will regard you as his patient even if you have never had to consult him. With the introduction of the system under which the National Health Service works people have become more and more doctor-conscious. In the old days when you had to pay cash for a consultation or run up a bill the doctor was normally called in only in cases of serious illness. And no doubt this was all to the good. Reliance on tablets and pills has made people forget about that wonderful doctor within who is always waiting to spring into action to help and to heal you, a doctor who works non-stop all round the clock to keep you fighting fit.

Some people seem to take a morbid pleasure in sitting in a doctor's waiting room. Before the days of the Health Service there might have been something to be got out of it. You were waiting to see someone whom you regarded as a friend, someone who knew your personal problems and who would have time to listen to your troubles. How different it all is now. As one patient goes out another goes in. Within a couple of minutes or so the doctor's hand will probably begin to move towards the bell and the patient will know that time is up. Out he goes with a sickening realisation that he has not got what he came in the hope of getting. Prescription in hand he then goes off to the chemist to spend more of his precious time waiting for something to be made up which will probably be a product of some firm of British or American drug manufacturers. The pill or tablet which the poor patient takes home with such a pathetic faith may be a mere placebo, in which case he might just as well have stayed at home. If the drug contains some powerful substance that does destroy bacteria the chances are that it will kill off the good germs with the bad ones thus depleting the natural health-promoting forces.

This is what happens to the soil when treated with chemical fertilisers and poisonous weed-killers. The elements in the soil which keep up the level of natural fertility are destroyed along with the weed seeds. And so it is with the body when its delicate balance is affected. We have got into the habit of thinking that all germs are harmful but this is not so. The system is swarming with beneficent germs doing their best to keep down the ones that are potentially dangerous. We should be kinder to all these friendly little germs that are working so hard to keep us well and we should spare a thought for them before swallowing something that is going to weaken them or put them out of action altogether.

Not only are good and bad germs alike destroyed by some of the drugs prescribed by the medical practitioner, but it often happens that alarming side-effects are experienced by the sufferer which leads him to fear that fresh complications have arisen. This in turn sends him off for yet another visit to the doctor when most probably he will be told that he is allergic to that particular drug. He will then be given another prescription for another drug which the doctor says will counteract the effect of the one he first prescribed. And so the vicious circle goes on, and the body has to put up yet another fight against another enemy. If instead of treating the effect the doctor in the first place had tried to get at the cause he might have sent his patient home with a few simple instructions which, if followed, would have brought about an improvement and eventually a cure. To feed down instead of feeding up; to give the stomach a rest so that other organs could be relieved of having to cope with the daily chores involved in dealing with toxic substances and left free to marshal their forces for promoting the health of the body as a whole.

Dr Vincent Nesfield, the discoverer of the purification of water by chlorine, a man who has spent seventy years of his life as a Harley Street surgeon, a bacteriologist and a practising physician, said recently that medicine as such was 90% placebo and 10% curative, and that 10% beneficial only if based on the remedial products of Nature's dispensaries. If that is the conclusion of a man who, because of his age and his special qualifications, can be said to have had more experience of the medical profession than any other living man, it is time that the whole question of medication came under serious review. There is little likelihood that this will come about by any official action. The reviewing must be done by the individual and there is evidence that there is a growing dissatisfaction with the conventional method of prescribing drugs to deal with disease. Many intelligent people are beginning to realise that there are other ways of treating the disorders of the body based on the conception of wholeness.

To heal is to make whole. This theme of wholeness seems to run right through the New Testament with its record of miraculous cures. The woman who was healed instantaneously when she pushed through a crowd and touched the hem of Christ's garment was told that it was her faith that had made her whole. In the case of the centurion's servant those who had gone to ask for help 'found the servant whole that had been sick' on their return to the house. To the leper who returned to give thanks for his healing Jesus said, 'Thy faith hath made thee whole'. And to the paralytic who rose from his bed and walked He said, 'Thy sins are forgiven thee'. He did not say that the muscles of his legs had been strengthened, but that his mental and spiritual transgressions had been cancelled out. This would appear to be a demonstration of the interaction of the different spheres of activity in which we exist. It is a dynamic illustration of the overlapping of the provinces of the doctor, the psychiatrist and the priest. To live harmoniously on every level is to achieve the balance of the wholeness which is health.

A study of how the body is able to mend its broken bones, manufacture its own antiseptics, regulate the actions of its organs, renew its tissues and maintain an arm of defence against microbial invasion leads to the conclusion that it has within it a built-in urge towards perfection. It is this biological urge that you should rely upon when something goes wrong. It is this urge that is responsible for the expulsion of pus from an abscess. It manifests itself as a bilious attack, a pain, a rash, a suppuration. All these disorders are signs not of sickness but of health because they prove the efficiency of the defensive forces of the body in repelling what is not wanted. There is a principle of rejection at work in you. The intrusion of foreign bodies is not tolerated. This is your protection. Whether it is a thorn in your finger or a germ in your lung, Nature will take steps to reject it or render it harmless. The pain or discomfort felt in the process is not so much a warning that there is something wrong as a reassurance that there is something right and that the doctor within is doing his job.

The failure of the heart transplant operations was a proof of the body's independent and intolerant attitude towards the introduction of a foreign organ into its nicely balanced economy. Its refusal to accept it was so determined that we were made to realise that the body could think for itself. How else could it demonstrate its basic principle of rejection. A skin graft can be done only with the patient's own skin. This is one more example of the intelligence of the body and of the fact that it has a mind of its own. The rejection is Nature saying 'No'. She always does when a fundamental law has been flouted. Veneral disease is Nature having the last word in the matter of sexual permissiveness after the brainwashers of the young and cranky sex-education in schools have done their worst.

The idea of the heart as being the seat of thoughts and of the emotions goes as far back as the chronicled history of mankind. The notion persists, not only in the flowery language of the poet and the visionary flights of the religious mystic, but in the ordinary phrases in common use. We speak of the dearest wish of the heart, of the dreams and desires of the heart, of losing one's heart when fascinated by something or someone and of love being an affair of the heart. So this extraordinary organ that belongs to you personally and cannot be successfully put into somebody else's body is something more than a muscular pump that beats at the rate of about 72 times a minute. Dr Philip Blaiberg's wife found that out to her cost when, after the operation performed by Dr Christian Barnard, her husband came home to be kept alive on drugs, a man whose very nature had changed. 'I felt his new heart did not love me,' said Mrs Blaiberg in an interview for publication in a magazine. A sad little testimony to the fact that body, soul and mind constitute a trinity, acting and interacting in a way that can never be examined by a surgeon or explained by a scientist.

The creative force that built you up out of a speck of protoplasm is surely capable of doing its own running repairs without any help from you in the way of medication. Your contribution to the successful maintenance of health is to keep the intake of toxic substances to the minimum and to eliminate them entirely so far as you are able. You can help by living as simply and as frugally as possible. Too many hot baths, hot meals and hot drinks, too many hours spent in a centrally heated atmosphere, too many sweets and cakes, too many cigarettes or too many alcoholic stimulants

—every form of over-indulgence brings its own particular retribution worked out through the chain of cause and effect over a period of time. As soon as you cease growing you need less food, so do not overload your stomach just for the pleasure of eating, especially if you do not do enough physically to work it off.

Re-educate your palate to appreciate plain, pure natural food, but do not become a bore to yourself or to those who have to cater for you. It is better to go without than to upset others by being faddy. Enjoy what you eat but do not make a serious business of it. The body is capable of dealing with a reasonable amount of even the wrong type of food. The real danger lies in overeating. It is surprising how little you can manage on. If you become hungry a spoonful of honey will restore your energy almost immediately. As you cannot carry a honeypot around with you it is wise to have some before starting out if you are subject to a sudden attack of hunger as so many people are who use up a lot of nervous energy. Avoid highly coloured fruit drinks. And forget about all those pints of water that are said to do you so much good. Consider your kidneys. They can do only so much at a time and it is doubtful whether there is any real goodness in tap water. Even an ice-cold spring is suspect these days when the artificial manure spread on the fields seeps through the earth to poison the underground streams.

All these considerations are important to remember if you are going to co-operate with that wonderful fellow, the doctor within, but the most important of all is the training of your mind towards a right attitude in the matter of health.

Above all you must never entertain thoughts of fear. Fear lowers the tone and the tempo of your metabolism. Fear paralyses the will and saps vitality. You cannot afford to be afraid of anything. Hold up your head and face everything that comes at you knowing that there is a power within you that is greater than anything that you may have to overcome.

Faith is creative. It builds up what fear tears down. Faith leaps over all obstacles. Christ said that it removes mountains and so it does: the mountains of difficulty and misfortune that confront the pilgrim on his progress through life. Mountains take on strange shapes. Sometimes they loom up in the form of a pain or as a problem, but whatever their size they shrink at the approach of faith. Faith in what? Faith in yourself and in the God who made you.

12

WILL TO BE WELL

Underneath the part of your mind which registers pain, fatigue or discomfort there is a power that wants you to be well. Remember this if ever you feel that you are fighting a losing battle against exhaustion or any form of mental, physical or nervous breakdown. When in this state you are like a pauper starving to death in a dark little garret not knowing that there is a box of precious jewels in the cellar.

Accept the stupendous fact of this power within you that wants you to be well. Do not argue about it. Do not ask yourself if it works or how it works. That is something you do not need to know in order to experience what it can do for you. Accept this great truth in a spirit of humility and gratitude. Jesus said that if you want to enter the kingdom of heaven you must come as a little child, and by 'the kingdom of heaven' He meant the life that can be experienced here and now, for did He not say that the kingdom was within you? Riches will not help you in this mysterious business of getting into the kingdom, nor will technological skill or intellectual brilliance. You must take off all your material trappings and strip yourself down to the child within you, the trustful innocent little child that sees with a clear eye things hidden from the worldly wise. When the Word was made flesh and God became man He came as something small enough to be put into a cattle trough. And that is what you must do if you wish to enter this wonderful kingdom of health, happiness and harmony. You must accept a diminishment of worldly status but you will gain more than you lose, for you will come into your full inheritance as a child of God, made in His image and likeness with all that those words imply. And the Open Sesame to the gate of the kingdom is the simple two-word declaration: I believe.

Faith will give you staying power to hold on in what, in a material sense, seems like a hopeless situation, but faith is not sufficient. It must be backed by the authority of the will and behind the will there must be desire. Before you can will to be well you must want to be well.

Invalidism has its attractions. In some cases it can be an escape from realism. The invalid finds himself at the centre of things, an object of interest and sympathy. He is removed from the demands and obligations of everyday life. This subtle temptation must be resisted with all the determination at your command. Whatever the nature of the complaint you must deny it any power over your real self, the ideal self within. Think of it as an evil dream from which you are about to awake. Affirm your true identity as a spiritual being made in the Divine image, a being which cannot be deformed, diseased or destroyed, allying yourself with the infinite life that sustains the universe.

When you have affirmed your desire to be well you must rally all the forces of the will, but there will be something inside you that wants to prevent you from making the effort. It is the easiest thing in the world to go slack, to let the spine sag and the shoulders drop because one of the basic flaws in human nature is a tendency to indolence. No wonder shrewd old Mother Church included slothfulness amongst the seven deadly sins. It is easier to give way to your condition than to make the effort of challenging its right to disturb or distress you.

Many aches and pains are of psychosomatic origin. Nervous tension can cause pain that leaves the body drained of all vitality. This is not imaginary. It is an actual condition, but in order to assert your supremacy over it you must deny it validity. Mind is master.

Talk to your pain. Tell it to go and insist upon an immediate obedience to your command. Be firm and expect relief, knowing that you are backed by the power within that wants you to be well. Make no concessions. Insist upon an absolute freedom from pain and settle for nothing less.

At the earliest possible moment set about organising an intestinal spring clean. Cut down on food and throw out the drugs. Fast if you can and give the body a real chance to concentrate on the job of getting rid of waste. You know how easy it is to accumulate rubbish in the house and the same applies to the body; yet how often does the poor old body get a chance to

D

cleanse and recondition itself? Day by day the liver, the lungs, the heart, the kidneys, the muscles and all the other physiological bits and pieces do their work and keep you alive, but it often happens that as we get older we give them more and more to do instead of less and less. Gradually, over the years, the deposits of poisonous substances build up and the stage becomes set for the onset of degeneration.

The successful maintenance of sound health of mind and body does not depend upon one thing in particular. It depends on a synthesis of habits connected with eating and drinking, exercise and relaxation, and of the mental attitude.

You may rightly ask how this can be applied to the treatment of killer diseases like cancer, bronchitis, heart disease. The answer is that the body as a whole is subject to the law of cause and effect. The cellular anarchy which we call cancer is the end result of some process of degeneration or imbalance. The swelling which proclaims the presence of a malignant growth is merely the point of culmination, the outward and visible sign that the body is making an effort to get rid of something that is inimical to its efficient working. The lawless turmoil of the cells, is all a part of the fight being put up by the system to correct what is wrong. When a surgical operation is performed the knife does not get at the causes of the disease, it merely removes the visible effects of it and in most cases surgery accelerates the development of fresh manifestations of malignancy.

Some of the millions spent on the National Health

Service should be devoted to the building and equipment of places where terminal cases of cancer, for which orthodox methods have failed to find a cure, could be treated in an experimental way. If there is nothing to be lost there is much to be gained in view of the fact that there are other ways of treating cancer not recognised by the medical hierarchy. There have been many examples of the success of the Nature Cure method under which the fighting powers of the body are marshalled scientifically to vanquish the marauding forces of disease. Autogenous vaccination is another method of treating cancer which is frowned on by the orthodox medico but which has been proved to be successful or partially successful. A prolongation of life without the aid of drugs is better than a premature death and surely worth having even if the cure is not absolutely permanent.

In any case it is an attempt to do something for a sufferer instead of filling him up with dope and sending him home to die.

Millions of pounds are collected for cancer research and thousands of doctors and scientists are engaged in trying to find the cause and the cure but progress is slow. Some of this money should be devoted to the tackling of this vast and terrible problem outside the field of medical orthodoxy. Courageous doctors who are working along these lines should be encouraged and not regarded as cranks.

The failure of medical science to conquer cancer is, in my opinion, attributable to two things: the conservatism of those whose responsibility it is to direct the work done at Lincoln's Inn Fields and the apathy of the public which contributes so large a share of the cost of maintaining that expensive centre of research. This apathetic attitude towards one of the worst killer diseases of all time is due partly to mental ostracism, an understandable human weakness. Cancer is something that can happen to other people but not to you. Such a possibility is unimaginable so, very rightly, you do not try to imagine. You give a donation to a fund for cancer research and having done this you are content to leave it to the experts. What you forget is that the experts are also human beings with human failings.

Specialisation in one field of medicine can narrow vision and impoverish imagination. Those who have devoted years to the sincere study of a particular disease with the help of millions of pounds' worth of equipment may not readily lay their minds open to consider properly other theories propounded by those who are working on different or even simple nonmedical lines.

The sophisticated and expensive paraphernalia with which the medical profession surrounds itself appears to the general public to be part of a mystique, and as more and more die of this apparently incurable disease people are, inevitably, beginning to ask questions. The infallibility of the expert is coming under suspicion.

Is every possible avenue of research being explored regardless of whether or not it ties up with the official line? When it is realised that there is as yet no cure for the common cold, let alone cancer, maybe we should put less blind faith in orthodox methods and investigate more closely curative treatments which lie on the other side of the fence.

The Minister of Health could do much to encourage new approaches to this question, but the nationalisation of medical services does not seem to have stimulated any noticeably progressive thinking in this field. In 1938 a doctor who had received successful treatment for cancer in the Edinburgh School of Natural Therapeutics wrote to Sir Kingsley Wood offering to furnish him with particulars of the cure, but he received a reply stating that 'the Minister was not disposed to take special action'. So much for the official response of over thirty years ago during which time deaths from cancer have increased as have the efforts of the researchers.

All this may have taken us a long way from the subject, which is the prevention of illness through the retraining of the subconscious mind, but there is a connecting link between prevention and cure. They are two aspects of the one thing. The natural powers of resistance which enable you to maintain health and prevent disease are the same powers that must be called into action when attacked by disease.

A mind that is in touch with the great Super-mind underlying all manifestations of life is bound to receive the constant refreshment of new and original ideas. If you place yourself daily in this stream of inspiration you will be able to help strengthen the forces of reform in the medical world thus making a personal contribution to a real advancement. So do not regard the preservation of your own health along these lines as something self-centred. In helping yourself you help others. Not only do you become a nicer, a more attractive person to live with, but you are consciously or unconsciously demonstrating the principles and the practices of victorious living. And you never know how many lives you may be influencing as you go quietly about your studies believing in your ideas and making them work.

If some of the foregoing seems too metaphysical and difficult to put into practice ignore the parts that do not make an appeal to your imagination, concentrating on what has an immediate effect upon you personally. Break it down into what is simple and easily assimilated.

Decide what it is that you want out of life and train your subconscious mind to shape it into actuality. Health, happiness, prosperity, peace, love. Whatever it is believe in your ability to achieve what you desire, but remember that it is dangerous to misuse the power of thought for purely personal and material advantages. You will get what you want but first be sure that you really want it. Make sure also that the fulfilment of this particular desire would not hurt somebody else or involve others in anything that would bring worry or unhappiness. Take your desires into the silence of prayer in a spirit of submission to the will of God remembering that there is plan for you in His purpose, which if worked out would lead to your ultimate good.

Affirm daily that you are evolving towards being the

sort of person you want to be. Picture yourself as being healthy, efficient and capable even if you feel unwell, incompetent and useless. Name the characteristics that you most admire in others and would wish to possess yourself and visualise circumstances in which you can see yourself as behaving according to these ideals.

When you have had a few moments of preparatory silence say verbally or mentally what it is that you wish to be or do. And while you are giving expression to your desires bring your imagination to bear upon the definite realisation of what you are affirming. If you want health realise that you are already in possession of health; it is already pouring through you in a life-giving stream, tingling into every pore and fibre of your being. Feel it surging through your veins, renewing and recharging you. If you are feeling lonely or unloved realise that you have within you the power of giving and of receiving love by reason of the fact that you are a child of infinite Love itself. There is an Entity to which you have access, a Power and a Presence that is, according to Alfred, Lord Tennyson, closer to you than breathing and nearer than hands and feet.

In the following pages suggestions are outlined for the wording of your affirmations, but as your experience deepens you will be able to formulate your desires in your own words. Even if results are not apparent immediately you are not wasting your time. You are building up mental reserves of strength and faith, making your soul and shaping your life. And this process does not stop when you rise from your chair at the conclusion of your daily meditation. Every thought must be brought into line with your intention and orientated towards the realisation of the ideal self.

Many branches of the arts of healing lie outside the citadel of orthodox medicine, homoeopathy, radiesthesia, psychotherapy, naturopathy, osteopathy, psychic and spiritual healing and Christian Science, but you must remember there is no panacea for all ills. Like the doctors, the unorthodox practitioners have their failures as well as their successes. This is because the healing power of God is transmitted through a human agency and nothing that is human can be perfect. Even so, never accept a hopeless diagnosis as final. Hold on to the hope that is in you and follow where it leads, willing to be well.

YES TO LIFE

Say Yes to Life and let it come
   Bounding into heart and home,
Giving all it has to give
   Say your Yes to Life and live.

Say No to Life and day by day
   The fire of it will die away
Leaving the ash for you to sieve,
   Working out your negative
In the grey world that you choose
   Saying No to God's good news,
Unfulfilled and unaware
   Of the glory everywhere.

Accept what comes, the boon, the bane,
   Impervious to loss or gain,
Looking forward, saying Yes
   To hope and health and happiness.

PATIENCE STRONG

Life is for Living

Thoughts for the daily meditation of those who
are
LONELY
AFRAID
FRUSTRATED
DISABLED
OVERWROUGHT
OVERBURDENED
DISAPPOINTED

LONELY

When I acknowledge the Fatherhood of God I am reminded that I am a member of a family and not an isolated individual left out in the cold. As I realise this truth I am brought into contact with like-minded people. The realisation that I belong to God's family works in me like a magnetic force which attracts into my orbit circumstances which dispel all sense of loneliness.

I am grateful for the blessings of friendships but am not dependent upon them for my peace and happiness. I cultivate a spirit of contentment, and starting every day in a mood of thankfulness I find more and more in life for which to be thankful.

As my dependence upon company grows less, I grow to cherish my hours of 'aloneness' realising that aloneness is not loneliness. 'Never less alone than when alone.' It is only in the times of quietude that I am able to develop my inner resources and come to know my true self. Much of what passes for social life is a waste of valuable time and I thank God for everything that gives me an opportunity of exploring the kingdom within.

Abide in me and I in you.   ST JOHN

AFRAID

I do not allow fear to cast its shadow over the sunshine of my day. Fear is the anticipation of an evil and I anticipate only good. Fear blanches the cheek, depresses the spirit and weakens the mind and I refuse to give it this power over me. Knowing that God is in control of His own universe and that I am a part of it I greet every morning with a declaration that all is well.

When I am in the grip of fear I attract to myself the very thing that I dread, so I replace fear with confidence. I am not afraid of anything because I know that if I co-operate with life it works in my favour and there is nothing to fear and no one of whom to be afraid.

If I allow my mind to become weakened by fear before a thing happens I have lost my battle before it has started. I wait before I worry knowing that if I have to face up to anything calamitous I shall be given strength according to my need and better able to cope with it if previously I have cultivated a confident and courageous spirit.

I will fear no evil.   PSALMS

FRUSTRATED

When things are not running smoothly for me I am inclined to give way to feelings of frustration, but this only makes matters worse. It is the point at which I must check up on my thinking and then I realise that I have been trying to work against instead of with the grain of life. Life is like a piece of living wood. The grain runs in a certain way and you have to work with it to get the best results. Life wants to work itself out harmoniously and successfully in and through me, but I must do my part and co-operate by not running counter to what I know to be wise and right.

When confronted with a difficult and seemingly hopeless situation I must pause, leaving it for the time being. It may be that I have been pulling in the wrong direction. My part is to take a hold on myself and know that everything will work out happily if I wait for it in a spirit of patience and confidence.

Fret not thyself.   PSALMS

DISABLED

Disablement does not mean defeat. I am not entirely dependent upon arms and legs for the living of my life. My real life goes on inside my mind and has its source of strength within my spirit. I live victoriously in my thoughts and my imagination.

God does not devise suffering but what He permits I must accept with grace and patience and within the framework of that acceptance I find that He has a mission for the sick and the handicapped. Successful living is not solely for the well and the active. By being cheerful, considerate and patient I can make a success of being an invalid, which in itself is an achievement.

I can depress others by being an object of pity or I can radiate a good humour which will make the healthy happy. The choice lies within myself. I can give in or I can fight on.

I must never cease to believe that I am getting better, but while I am as I am I will make the best of it. I will live above my afflictions and wrest a blessing out of adversity. I contemplate in quietness the beauty of trees, stars and clouds framed by my window, seeing more than those who hurry by too busy to look.

Rejoicing in hope, patient in tribulation.   ROMANS

OVERWROUGHT

The violinist knows how to tune his instrument to the required pitch, but if a string is overstrained it will snap at its weakest part. So it is with the delicately adjusted balance of the nervous system. One small additional worry will in some cases bring about a breakdown of the whole personality if the mind is already overwrought.

I must train myself to master circumstances or they will master me and this I cannot accomplish in my own strength. I need God.

There is a connection between empty churches and overcrowded mental hospitals. The human mind has not yet adapted itself to the speed, the noise and the horrors of our so-called civilisation. It still needs the peace that can be found only in communion with the supernatural and the unseen. Religion alone meets this need. We are told in the Bible to 'rest in the Lord'. In other words, relax in the Lord.

I need that kind of regular relaxation tossed about as I am in the cross currents of daily living. The psychiatrist with his verbal probings and the doctor with his drugs cannot cure this modern disease of mental breakdown, so I must never allow myself to become overwrought. I will prevent this crisis by doing the elementary exercises of practical psychology: being still and knowing that God is God.

They that wait upon the Lord shall renew their strength.
ISAIAH

OVERBURDENED

I must strengthen my spine for the shouldering of the burdens of life. I must not evade my responsibilities by saying that I am overworked, nor must I try to put my burden on somebody else's back. God never allows us to carry a load that we have not the strength to bear. When I realise this I find that there is always time to do what must be done and courage to bear what must be borne.

Sometimes when the going is tough I am inclined to give way to self-pity but I must learn to fight this insidious temptation and to be grateful for the opportunity of being useful. I must be an asset to the world in which I live and not a liability. I must tackle my own problems and bear my own burdens for how else can I grow to the full stature of my potentialities? But I cannot do this without a sustaining faith in a God upon whom I can lean. When I have this invisible support I never stumble under the weight of my cares. I run with them.

I perform every duty and I do every job that I see needs doing. I am never too busy or too tired to take on one more thing because 'I can do all things through

Christ who strengthens me'. I greet every morning with a grateful heart saying, 'Here am I, Lord, ready for anything'.

Come unto me all ye that labour and are heavy laden and I will refresh you. MATTHEW

DISAPPOINTED

When things do not work out as I plan and hopes come crashing to the ground I must never cease to affirm that behind all the frustrations of life there is a Power that is working everything out for my ultimate good.

When I do not get what I want or when I run up against unforeseen circumstances I must not give way to feelings of bitterness or to the foolish conclusion that I am unlucky. The suffering caused by disappointment is like the pain of a burst abscess. The exudation of pus is a sign that the body is healthy and able to reject what is not for its good and disappointment is also a crisis of rejection. It is life asserting itself on my behalf and refusing to allow something that is not in my best interests.

I must learn to accept all disappointments great and small with a philosophic calm, reaffirming the fact that there is an overruling Providence at work in all my affairs which is favourable and beneficent. Rebellion is defeat; acceptance is victory.

All things work together for good to them that love God.
ROMANS

117

Suggestions for the daily affirmation of
                    HEALTH
                    HARMONY
                    HAPPINESS
                    WISDOM
                    PEACE
                    LOVE
                    PROSPERITY

Because they are basic for the wholeness and well-being of every individual, regardless of circumstances, it is suggested that one only of these seven creative words be concentrated on for two or three consecutive days in order to impress them more effectively upon the subconscious mind.

As the student of practical psychology progresses in the demonstration of its principles he will be able to compose his own affirmations relevant to personal needs.

HEALTH

THERE IS A POWER WITHIN ME welling up from the deep reservoirs of life itself and I draw now upon this power for the health and healing of mind and body. Quietly and with confidence I rest upon the knowledge that because I am made in the image and likeness of my Creator I am in my true self capable of being and becoming whole and healthy.

In order to experience and to enjoy this to the full I must be rid of all mental and physical impurities. My soul must be fed upon the bread of faith and my body strengthened by a mind which is positive in its outlook, cheerful and resilient.

Resisting anything which tends to undermine belief in this wonderful potentiality within, I refuse to entertain thoughts in which I appear as sick, weak or disabled and I do not allow my tongue to dwell upon physical defects and diseases. My thinking and my speaking reflect only that which is good, hopeful and healthy.

I thank God daily for every blessing. I claim my birthright as His child and accept with joy my Divine endowment of health and wholeness.

Be ye transformed by the renewing of your mind.   ROMANS

HARMONY

THERE IS A POWER WITHIN ME that is able to bring harmony into my life at every level of living. Where there is strife the whole situation can be changed by the introduction of a note that softens the sharp edge of discord. Harmony in music is produced when different notes are brought together into a natural and right relationship and the same laws of harmony operate in life as in music. One of the secrets of maintaining harmonious relationships with other people is knowing how and when to strike the right note.

As I go through my day with all its difficulties I try to remember that underneath the superficial conflicts and confusions there is this law of harmony at work waiting to be brought into operation. I create harmony every time I refuse to react adversely to the provocations of opposition. Thus do I affirm its reality. By holding to this thought and speaking only the tranquillising word I change the tone.

My body also comes under the laws of harmony for every organ must function harmoniously if perfect health is to be enjoyed.

A word spoken in due season, how good it is. PROVERBS

HAPPINESS

THERE IS A POWER WITHIN ME that, whenever I open my mind to it, is able to flood my whole being with happiness because it springs from the eternal sources of pure joy. This joy reaches me through various channels: music, beauty, poetry, friendship, love, but it is through communion with the living Christ that I experience the supreme joy: the joy that is beyond all telling. Paradoxically, it was the Man of Sorrows who said, 'My joy no man taketh from you'.

I do not feel guilty at being happy in an unhappy world because the injunction to rejoice runs right through my Bible like a golden thread. The fact that I am able at any time to draw upon this inexhaustible well of happiness proves that it is something which is always flowing from God to man.

I cultivate a happy attitude towards life because in so doing I radiate a power which attracts happy circumstances and repels what is adverse and unhappy. In the beautiful first collect for Advent I am told to put on the armour of light and this I do when I face the day in a happy and optimistic frame of mind.

THERE IS A POWER WITHIN ME WHICH IS PURE JOY
In thy presence is fulness of joy; at thy right hand are pleasures for evermore.   PSALMS

WISDOM

THERE IS A POWER WITHIN ME that is infinite wisdom itself. It lies beneath the level of the intellect and is the hidden spring of all true wisdom. Insight and intuition come not from the objective mind with its jumbled store of facts and fantasies, but from below the subconscious where lie the deep sources of Divine intelligence.

I feed my mind continually with the wise words of Holy Scripture which creates reserves of wisdom on which I can draw in time of need. As I become receptive to its promptings I find that I rely more and more upon this inner wisdom for guidance and understanding and less and less upon my own superficial impulses.

I trust the Supreme Wisdom to give me the right answer at the right moment and in order to become a clear channel for the inflowing of this intuitive knowledge I try to reduce the complicated business of living to its simplest terms.

The natural man receiveth not the things of the spirit, neither can he know them because they are spiritually discerned. CORINTHIANS

PEACE

THERE IS A POWER WITHIN ME that permeates my whole being with a deep sense of peace. This peace is something more than a mere absence of noise or cessation of movement. It is creative and restorative. In the midst of turmoil I can make a stillness within myself and withdraw into this secret refuge to recharge and relax.

I carry this peace with me through the business of the day and am armoured against disturbing and destructive elements. In a world of strife and turbulence I open my mind to the awareness of this peace wherever I may be and its quiet influence flows out to disarm the quarrelsome spirit. In its power I am able to speak the word that calms troubled waters.

I claim now the Divine legacy left to me personally by the Master when He said, 'My peace I leave with you, my peace I give unto you'.

Be still and know that I am God.   PSALMS

LOVE

THERE IS A POWER WITHIN ME that is love and this links me directly with God Himself for, in the words of St John, 'God is Love'. The only thing that really matters in life is knowing how to receive and give love. Love in its deepest Christian sense goes beyond mere personal attachments. In its highest manifestation it is impersonal, so I must strive to cultivate and to practise the kind of love that will embrace even those whom I dislike. To subdue prejudices and emotions and to deal lovingly with strangers, acquaintances and enemies is to share in God's work of reconciliation between man and man. Love can never withhold good, nor can it wish to hurt or impoverish.

I dwell in thought upon the amazing truth that God loves me. As His child I am a member of the royal family of the King of Heaven. Claiming my Divine birthright I live in the enjoyment of all that He bestows upon me as a loving Father. This love encircles the world and within this circle I am related to every member of the human family. Knowing this I must bear no malice or think no evil of anyone, remembering the message of the Bethlehem angels: goodwill toward men.

Love one another.   ST PETER

PROSPERITY

THERE IS A POWER WITHIN ME that is able to supply my every need. Lack of any of the necessities of life implies a lack of faith. God is a great giver and He withholds from me nothing that is essential for my ultimate good. I do not desire more than I can use, nor do I desire luxury or outward show, but only that which contributes to my well-being, mental, spiritual and physical.

All things wholesome and beautiful serve to enrich life. Said Jesus, 'I am come that they might have life and have it more abundantly'. Whatever I desire comes to me by force of attraction if I hold to it in a spirit of expectation, so I desire not worldly but spiritual prosperity. This encompasses all that is required for the living of a rich and satisfying life on every plane of experience. As I learn to live frugally and with simplicity I become more and more aware of my prosperity in the true sense of the word because I know that at any time I can draw upon the immense reserves of a beneficent providence.

I am a steward for whatever money comes into my possession, and I know intuitively what to give and what to retain. Giving keeps open the channels of blessing. The more I give the richer I grow. I do not have to be wealthy in order to feel prosperous, for real prosperity is an attitude of mind.

The Lord is my shepherd. I shall not want.   PSALMS